VALERIE ESTELLE FRANKEL

WHO TELLS YOUR STORY?

Other Works by Valerie Estelle Frankel

Henry Potty and the Pet Rock: A Harry Potter Parody
Henry Potty and the Deathly Paper Shortage: A Harry Potter Parody
Buffy and the Heroine's Journey
From Girl to Goddess: The Heroine's Journey in Myth and Legend
Katniss the Cattail: The Unauthorized Guide to Name and Symbols
The Many Faces of Katniss Everdeen: The Heroine of The Hunger Games
Harry Potter, Still Recruiting: A Look at Harry Potter Fandom
Teaching with Harry Potter
An Unexpected Parody: The Spoof of The Hobbit Movie
Teaching with Harry Potter
Myths and Motifs in The Mortal Instruments
Winning the Game of Thrones: The Host of Characters & their Agendas
Winter is Coming: Symbols, Portents, and Hidden Meanings in A Game of Thrones
Bloodsuckers on the Bayou: The Myths, Symbols, and Tales Behind HBO's True Blood
The Girl's Guide to the Heroine's Journey
Choosing to be Insurgent or Allegiant: Symbols, Themes & Analysis of the Divergent Trilogy
Doctor Who and the Hero's Journey: The Doctor and Companions as Chosen Ones
Doctor Who: The What Where and How
Sherlock: Every Canon Reference You May Have Missed in BBC's Series
Symbols in Game of Thrones
How Game of Thrones Will End
Joss Whedon's Names
Pop Culture in the Whedonverse
Women in Game of Thrones: Power, Conformity, and Resistance
History, Homages and the Highlands: An Outlander Guide
The Catch-Up Guide to Doctor Who
Remember All Their Faces: A Deeper Look at Character, Gender and the Prison World of Orange Is The New Black
Everything I Learned in Life I Know from Joss Whedon
Empowered: The Symbolism, Feminism, & Superheroism of Wonder Woman
The Avengers Face their Dark Sides
The Comics of Joss Whedon: Critical Essays
Mythology in Game of Thrones
We're Home: Fandom, Fun, and Hidden Homages in Star Wars the Force Awakens

WHO TELLS YOUR STORY?

History, Pop Culture, and Hidden Meanings in the Musical Phenomenon Hamilton

by
Valerie Estelle Frankel

Who Tells Your Story is an unauthorized guide to *Hamilton: An American Musical* and related works. None of the individuals or companies associated with this series or any merchandise based on this series has in any way sponsored, approved, endorsed, or authorized this book.

ISBN-13: 978-1541115217
ISBN-10: 154111521X

FOR MY GRANDFATHER, HARRY
KANTER, WHO ADORED MUSICALS – IF
IT'S A GOOD ONE, HE SAID, YOU'LL LEAVE
IT SINGING.

CONTENTS

INTRODUCTION

"How did a chapter of U.S. history you more than likely slept through become a pop-culture phenomenon to rival *Star Wars*?" (Berman)

It all began when Lin-Manuel Miranda, creator of the Tony Award winning musical *In the Heights* took Chernow's weighty 2004 biography of Alexander Hamilton on vacation as a beach read. By the second chapter of the book he was inspired ("Hip-hop and History Blend").

Ron Chernow explains, "I think that this is a classic immigrant story in terms of someone recognizing the opportunities in this brand new turbulent wide-open society…I daresay [Hamilton] made the greatest contribution of any immigrant in the history of the United States" ("Hamilton: A Founding Father"). Reading about the Founding Father, Miranda saw his own father journeying to a new land and himself struggling to write his way into fame and fortune…and succeeding.

On May 12, 2009, Miranda was invited to perform from *In the Heights* at the White House before President Obama. Instead, he chose to perform the one rap he'd written – the opening number. As he said, he wanted to celebrate "someone who embodies hip-hop, Treasury Secretary Alexander Hamilton," and the room laughed. However, they were soon swept away. Obama gave him a standing ovation and the *YouTube* video went viral. Miranda says of that event:

> I felt like I was meeting a moment. This was a president that I had worked hard to help elect, and I wanted to show something about the American experience and do

something new there because I felt like I was part of
something. (DiGiacomo)

"Today, that song is the opening number of a show that
uses mostly actors of color to play 'old, dead white men,' as
Miranda puts it, and hip-hop, R&B and pop to tell the story
of Hamilton's life and death" (DiGiacomo).

By 2015, he'd written the musical and was performing in
it at the Public Theatre off-Broadway with a cast of other
groundbreaking performers.

There are nearly 50 songs in *Hamilton* (though its Playbill
lists only 34) and it's entirely a musical of lyrics, with very few
lines simply spoken. SpotCo's Nicky Lindeman explains that
the show's now familiar logo uses the star from the American
flag. "The black star and the black silhouette were a nod to
portraits of the period, but merged together they seemed like
a modern image" – which feels like an apt metaphor for the
show itself (Mandell).

> Having already set sales and awards benchmarks for a
> Broadway show – $111 million in ticket sales in just over 13
> months, 16 Tony Award nominations (and 11 wins), a
> Pulitzer Prize for Drama – *Hamilton* has leaped off the
> stage and become a full-blown cultural phenomenon.
> (Berman)

On describing his success, Miranda modestly comments,
"I knew we'd be a hit with history teachers. Everything else
has been sort of a surprise" (Kokalitcheva).

Nonetheless, his passion project succeeded, recasting the
Founding Fathers with actors of color like himself and his
gifted rapper friends, establishing a visual and auditory picture
of Revolutionary America much more in keeping with
America of today.

This book explores the show's deeper symbols and
meanings, from the staging to the dances, and considers how
it all enhances the meaning. There's the ship scaffolding
scenery that builds as America does. Recurring motifs echo –

private and public life, legacy, memory, heroism, villainy, and how all of these will be recorded for the future. There are so many implications for "shot" or "satisfied," so many nods to the audience and to the works of rap, hip-hop, and musical theater that inspired the show. Through it all, plenty of moments "break the fourth wall," reminding the audience it's a work of fiction.

There are also the characters – Washington as father-figure, Angelica and Eliza as contrasting female sides that echo mind and heart, Laurens/Philip as idealism, and of course, Burr as ever-present reflection of the hero. All these offer secrets and surprises as Hamilton's story reflects in so many ways the America of today and its diverse, creative citizens.

A CLOSE READING OF THE MUSICAL – HISTORY, THEMES, SYMBOLS, STAGING, & DEEPER MEANINGS

ACT I

History: Birth to Arrival

How does a bastard, orphan, son of a whore and a
Scotsman, dropped in the middle of a
Forgotten spot in the Caribbean by Providence
Impoverished, in squalor
Grow up to be a hero and a scholar?

Aaron Burr asks this provocative question as narrator,
opening the show – it's a surprising story and the musical will
actually undertake to answer the question through the
narrative of Hamilton's life. At the same time, this is a
question the more cultured Burr truly seeks to know – how
did this foreigner beat him in so many ways? Thus the
provocative hook for the audience is also a tease on his own
character and the ongoing rivalry that will come.

"The story of the life of Alexander Hamilton is a story
that the most gifted novelist could not have invented. Too
much of it would seem implausible in terms of what
happened to this man in the space of forty-nine years. I
mean, it's just better than any novel," remarks Ron Chernow,
whose biography *Alexander Hamilton* inspired Lin-Manuel
Miranda's musical (*Alexander Hamilton: American Experience*).

Unlike the other founding fathers, Alexander Hamilton
was an outsider, born in 1755 on Nevis, a tiny tropical island
in the Caribbean. He was also the youngest of them. Author
Willard Sterne Randall adds, "Hamilton's the only one of the
Founding Fathers who was an outsider, an orphan, an
immigrant, a scholarship boy, a college dropout" (*Alexander*

17

VALERIE ESTELLE FRANKEL

Hamilton: American Experience). Throughout his life, criticism
would suggest that he was part Black, part Creole, and so
forth. He was also stigmatized for being a bastard, as his
mother had left his Scottish father. Chernow explains:

> It's hard for us to transport ourselves back to a time in the
> eighteenth century when everything revolved around birth
> and breeding and pedigree. I think that the illegitimacy had
> the most profound effect, psychologically, on Hamilton. It
> was considered the most dishonored state, and I think that
> it produced in Hamilton a lifelong obsession with honor.
> (*Alexander Hamilton: American Experience*)

The opening number "Alexander Hamilton" has the main
characters all in white including Hamilton himself,
emphasizing that they've stepped from the pages of a book or
out of the mists of history. Only Burr, the central narrator of
this piece, keeps his red coat, suggesting power, pride, and
battle as well as a vital role here – more vital in some ways
than Hamilton's. Spotlights hit one character at a time,
inviting them to give their short rap speech then blink out of
history for a time. Each introduces himself and his relation to
the hero. The lights slowly rise to fill in the ship-scaffolding
set even as Hamilton plans to embark for the world of
opportunity.

The ensemble's women in white corsets and breeches
look androgynous as they're wearing about the same thing as
the men. It's oddly sexy, given that this would have been
underwear at the time but now counts as modest covering.
The men, in their white waistcoats and breeches, likewise
suggest they're wearing underwear – gentlemen never went
bare armed at this time. Black boots and black collars add a
bit of contrast, making the whiteness glow even more.
Despite this, the paleness emphasizes lack of personality as
they're the anonymous crowd.

In the scene, several mime the hero's dying mother and
cousin, adding to their ghostly aspect. Further, in this
number, the ensemble is joined by the apparitions of

18

historical figures, dead by the story's end.

The ghostliness of the cast echoes the tragedy and loss in the historical Hamilton's life – his family quickly became only memories. Around the age of thirteen, he lost his mother to yellow fever. His father had already left two years before. He went to live with a first cousin who committed suicide a year later. Chernow adds, "These experiences would have shattered a lesser individual. But all of these misfortunes actually toughen this spirit of self-reliance. He realized that his great asset was his intelligence, which he would have to do everything to develop" (*Alexander Hamilton: American Experience*).

The only thing Hamilton managed to keep from his mother's very modest estate was the books, which no one valued but him, "retreatin' and readin' every treatise on the shelf" and "scammin' for every book he can get his hands on." With these words, the ensemble all greedily snatch up books from a desk, emphasizing Hamilton's desperation for them. This also links his story with the larger world of story in general – today we know about Hamilton's life from books, which were used to create this musical.

At age fourteen, Hamilton became a clerk for the American firm of Beekman and Cruger and learned much about currency. Author Willard Sterne Randall explains:

> Hamilton, as a teenager, had to become a master of international currencies. There was no one currency. He had to know the exchange rates: Dutch, Portuguese, Spanish, French, English, et cetera. He had to be an evaluator, an appraiser, a moneychanger. And so he learned a great deal about trade in a very short time. (*Alexander Hamilton: American Experience*)

While he ran the firm for its sick owner and dictated to people far older than he was, he also witnessed the brutality of buying slaves to work the sugar cane fields. He empathized with them as he felt they and he were wasted in obscurity. He wrote to his friend Edward Stevens:

> To confess my weakness, Ned, my ambition is so prevalent that I disdain the groveling conditions of a clerk to which my fortune condemns me. I would willingly risk my life, though not my character, to exalt my station. My folly makes me ashamed, yet Neddy, we know that such schemes can triumph when the schemer is resolute. Oh, how I wish there was a war! (*Alexander Hamilton: American Experience*)

The war of course was soon to come. By 1772, the teenager was not only running a major shipping company, but also writing articles. One, on the devastation of a hurricane, caught people's eye and several influential people funded a scholarship for the lad to King's College, later to become Columbia University.

When he discovers his destiny in the musical, the tempo doubles. As Miranda explains, "The image in my head is of Harry Potter finding out he's a wizard. Everything finally makes sense" (*Hamilton: The Revolution* 17). He arrives in New York in 1773 with much to prove. As he sings in "My Shot":

> I'm 'a get a scholarship to King's College
> I prob'ly shouldn't brag, but dag, I amaze and astonish
> The problem is I got a lot of brains but no polish

"He chose a psychological strategy adopted by many orphans and immigrants: he decided to cut himself off from his past and form a new identity. He would find a home where he would be accepted for that he did, not for who he was" (Chernow 40). To historian Gordon S. Wood

> He has this chip on his shoulder, precisely because of his background, his illegitimacy. He's going to show the world that he's not going to suffer any disrespect from anyone, especially given his talent, which he knows he has – and he's not hiding it under any bushels either. (*Alexander Hamilton: American Experience*)

Suggesting he's about to play a role, the onstage Hamilton removes his white coat and dons a brown one offered to him by Eliza, his personal seamstress and homemaker. He hands the white coat to Burr, emphasizing his antagonist's role as helper in this biography. (Throughout Act I, he will switch coats over a white suit, emphasizing his many life roles – innocent, New Yorker, soldier, politician.) His beloved Angelica gives him books, equipping him for the trip and hinting at their future witty correspondence. If he is on a hero's journey, they, not his sword, will be his talismans and weapons. Laurens gives him a travel bag that might also suggest his soldier's kit – he and Laurens will be aides-de-camp together.

The stairs descend, suggesting a set being fashioned around him. The lyric, "We are waiting in the wings for you" likewise emphasizes his life as theater production. Likewise, "Just you wait" works as commentary on his life as well as an instruction to the audience. There's a great deal of punning, double meanings, and clever language ("New York"/"new man"), setting the tone for the entire show. Set designer David Korins adds, "What I knew very early on was that we were going to throw some sort of theatrical metaphor wrapping so that we would take no time transitioning from one location to the next. There are moments in the show where it breaks into abstract realism or moments of pure abstraction" (Eddy). The ship-city is sometimes both, sometimes neither – the question from moment to moment is who is captaining it.

The stage back includes a partially built brick wall, to which more feet are added during intermission, symbolizing the building of the country. Most of the set is wooden scaffolding of a sort. Korins continues:

> We came up with a couple of different ideas. One was that the surround was a theatrical metaphor of sorts for what was actually happening at the time in the country. It is architecturally like a tapestry of early American architecture. At that time, the carpenters were actually ship builders. The building methodologies they employed were ones of boat builders. We carried that into our set, you see all of the

seams and all the joints that made up all the boards and beams, all come from ship building techniques. There's a lot of rope, block and tackle, pulleys and other nautical references... We're not building the inside dome of the Capitol. We're not building the Washington Monument. What we're doing is we are building the kind of structure that is the scaffolding and the wrapping that we then will build all these things from. (Eddy)

Mulligan, Lafayette, Laurens, and Washington summarize the story to come, like a Greek chorus or Shakespearean prologue, thus giving an old-fashioned convention to the story as they set up how their lives intersected. The double roles mean that Madison, Jefferson, and Philip appear here as well. The former two's "We fought with him" references fighting beside him in the war then literally fighting with him over policy, in one of the show's clever double entendres. Laurens as well as Philip thus says the line "Me? I died for him." As the number ends, Washington and Laurens/Phillip are lit with white ghostly light far in the background while Burr in his red coat glows as narrator.

As the crowd dances, Burr meets Hamilton at the foot of the gangplank, welcoming him to a new city. "The ship is in the harbor now/See if you can spot him," Burr sings as Hamilton vanishes into the crowd. Upon his arrival, he is just one more immigrant in New York.

On his line confessing "I'm the damn fool that shot him," Burr is center stage, full in the spotlight and looking sheepish. Burr starts forward, but stumbles at Hamilton comes up from behind him and takes his place (more symbolism for how events will transpire). "What's your name, man?"

"Alexander Hamilton."

On the Double Roles

Double roles add character depth. Lafayette is the French outsider who's nonetheless a close friend – the one Hamilton high-fives on "Immigrants – we get the job done!" In Act II, casting him as Jefferson stresses the latter character's French sophistication and outsider status once again – Jefferson did not fight in the war but is butting into the new country's policies nonetheless. As he's Hamilton's political rival, he contrasts with his previous role of close friend. Further, Lafayette's loyal determination to make the war succeed then spread freedom to his own country clashes with Jefferson's privileged demands that all of America conform to his view – the gentleman farmer undesirous of a national treasury or slave emancipation. Nonetheless, both are patriots, driven by their conviction and both ardently support the French Revolution. There's extra meaning when Jefferson insists the new country should aid Lafayette, though Hamilton and Washington refuse this last plea from an old friend.

Okieriete Onaodowan transforms a great deal: In Act One he's the muscle; in Act Two the brains. "As Hamilton's friend Hercules Mulligan, Oak rapped in a booming growl and pretended that he had trouble controlling his powerful limbs; as James Madison, he shrank his 5'11", 235-pound frame, and adopted a nasal voice, diminishing himself to play Jefferson's shy, sickly partner" (*Hamilton: The Revolution*, 148).

Mulligan/Madison turns from revolutionary friend to political enemy, though both of these are insiders. These two are inverted as Mulligan is a rebel with piles of attitude – someone high schoolers see themselves reflected in. He hurtles into the rebellion, doing a magnificent leap on "Rise up!" The Madison of the musical is a "yes man" who only exists to push Jefferson into battling Hamilton in debate – a far quieter figure in grey. As Jefferson's sidekick, he's manipulative but near-silent. As such, he suggests the transformation some men undergo when the revolution has concluded, changing from warriors to cautious politicians.

Laurens/Philip shows Hamilton's son growing up as beloved as the best friend of his youth, both tragically destined to die young. Both have a great deal of idealism, with a selfless love for others (from the slaves to Philip's family to Hamilton himself). Laurens historically was Hamilton's closest companion, whose death he never got over (much like his son's). "During Laurens's Southern sojourn, Hamilton wrote to him some of the most personally revealing letters of his life." In one April 1779 letter, Hamilton expressed such fervent and open affection for Laurens that Hamilton's son wrote a note that he "must not publish the whole of this" (Chernow 123). As the letter goes:

> Cold in my professions, warm in [my] friendships, I wish, my Dear Laurens, it m[ight] be in my power, by action rather than words, [to] convince you that I love you. I shall only tell you that 'till you bade us Adieu, I hardly knew the value you had taught my heart to set upon you. Indeed, my friend, it was not well done. You know the opinion I entertain of mankind, and how much it is my desire to preserve myself free from particular attachments, and to keep my happiness independent on the caprice of others. You sh[ould] not have taken advantage of my sensibility to ste[al] into my affections without my consent. But as you have done it and as we are generally indulgent to those we love, I shall not scruple to pardon the fraud you have committed, on condition that for my sake, if not for your own, you will always continue to merit the partiality, which you have so artfully instilled into [me]. (*Papers of Alexander Hamilton*, vol. 2, p. 34).

Conventions of the time were different, but even if this is not a letter of romantic love, it describes a true bosom companion. Hamilton wrote little on either loss, letting the silence describe his devastation more than anything. Likewise, on the show, he cannot react to the shock of Laurens' sudden death, insisting instead, "I have so much work to do" and burying himself in the job. By contrast, at Philip's passing he stops, only wandering the empty streets, unable to phrase his loss in words. "There are moments that the words don't reach/There is suffering too terrible to name," the lyrics insist, but Angelica must voice them for a devastated Hamilton. Each of these losses destroys him personally and hardens him for the political decisions he must make.

Peggy, the sweet third sister (admittedly with little to do) is recast as treacherous Maria, adding a touch of extra incest and betrayal to the forbidden tryst. The shyest, Peggy interrupts "The Schuyler Sisters" as they explore New York with "Daddy said to be home by sundown" and "Daddy said not to go downtown" as a clearly obedient "daddy's girl." Like her, Maria is the servant of the patriarchy, following her husband's instructions to seduce Hamilton for profit, then cringing before her lover. Chernow adds, "Whatever Maria Reynolds's initial intentions, Hamilton must have seemed elegant, charming, and godlike compared to her vulgarian husband" (366). Both are helpless ninnies but set in opposition as saint and Jezebel.

Washington has no double role, making him and Burr fundamental pillars of the story, who accompany Hamilton from prologue to first act to second, much as Eliza and Angelica do. All narrate his story and also help usher him into renown and then death.

A Jungian interpretation has Hamilton as hero with all the other characters voicing parts of his personality – Washington represents fatherly advice and experienced wisdom, like Yoda. The loss of Hamilton's mother fills him with survivor guilt and despair, as seen in "Hurricane." Gentle Laurens, who dreams of a world without slavery, is like Hamilton's naiveté – with the same actor playing his son, both characters embody his grand hopes for all the new country can be. Both, of course, soon perish. Mulligan is Hamilton's adventure spirit, and Lafayette, his potential, as both become war heroes and guide Hamilton to do the same. However, in the gloomier Act II, the pair are directly replaced by Hamilton's political rivals, now scheming to bring him down instead of raise him up. In the same way that Frodo's cheerful cousins, Merry and Pippin, give place to the scheming Gollum in *The Lord of the Rings*, Hamilton has entered a darker story and his companions tempt him into despair. Nonetheless, these friends all help teach him about what it means to be a patriot. As Jung adds, "Once one has experienced a few times what it is like to stand judgingly between the opposites, one begins to understand what is meant by the self" (*Civilization in Transition*, 872).

Eliza and Angelica are like two halves of the ideal woman, one a motherly comforter and one a challenging, witty flirt. In the musical and in history, the two women exert different types of pull on him.

> Together the two eldest sisters formed a complete portrait of Hamilton's ideal woman, each appealing to a different facet of his personality. Eliza reflected Hamilton's earnest sense of purpose, determination, and moral rectitude, while Angelica exhibited his worldly side – the wit, charm, and vivacity that so delighted people. (Chernow 133)

Each challenges him to grow and improves him through her love…though the personalities are so different. Both in Jungian terms are the anima – the inner woman who helps the hero discover love and the spiritual world of home and family, not just politics. In Act II, sweet, childish Peggy is replaced by the scheming seductress Maria (again creating a darker story) and thus optimistic Eliza turns melancholy and despondent, even before their real loss. Hamilton's spiritual side despairs, and he must win it back. As Jung notes, "Permanent loss of the anima means a diminution of vitality, of flexibility and of human kindness. The result, as a rule, is premature rigidity, crustiness, stereotypy, fanatical one-sidedness, obstinacy, pedantry" ("Concerning the Archetypes" 71). Hamilton temporarily descends into this darkness after losing Eliza and Angelica both, but woos the women and their gentle grace back before his death. Even after it, Eliza continues as his savior, redeeming his public image and keeping his legacy alive.

Burr is the shadow – all of Hamilton's fears that he's being too impulsive, too bold, and that these attempts to better himself will destroy him. Jung writes: "The shadow personifies everything that the subject refuses to acknowledge about himself and yet is always thrusting itself upon him directly or indirectly—for instance, inferior traits of character and other incompatible tendencies" (*Archetypes and Collective Unconscious* 285). Burr and Hamilton, like Elphaba and Glinda in *Wicked*, are enticed and repelled on sight, as each is what the other could have been with different choices. Each time they meet, it's a reminder of missed opportunities – each embraces what the other rejects.

Aaron Burr, Sir

"Pardon me. Are you Aaron Burr, sir?" Hamilton asks, starting the rhyme pattern that will last through the musical. Burr, his future nemesis, is the first friend he makes in the musical. Miranda has called this "basically Harry Potter meeting Draco Malfoy" (*Hamilton: The Revolution* 24) and indeed, in both stories, this nemesis functions as a guide to the new world, though his philosophies contrast with the hero's so much that the hero rejects this advice. Thus the audience is presented with a truth besides the hero's – one can make friends genuinely and speak from the heart or watch one's words and seek opportunities for advancement (this summation actually works for both stories, comparing the straightforwardly honest hero with the conniving social climber). Burr's role as narrator echoes Judas's in *Jesus Christ: Superstar* – the hero's tale is told from the villain's point of view, but the latter becomes in many ways more relatable.

> Hip-hop wins sympathy for the bad guy in a more aggressive, pummeling way. It's also often a stinging complaint against injustice. Maybe that's why Aaron Burr seems so compelling in *Hamilton*. He opens the show, vehemently rapping his grievances about the unfairness of his situation. How did Hamilton, of all people, he asks, a "bastard, orphan son of a whore and a Scotsman," dropped in the middle of forgotten spot in the Caribbean, grow to be a "hero and a scholar?" (Tommasini and Caramanica)

Burr's frequent "how" and "why," stress how perplexed he is by the events he's narrating. His line "How does an orphan…" or variations on this (beginning "Alexander

Hamilton," "A Winter's Ball," "Guns and Ships," "What'd I Miss," "The Adams Administration," and "Your Obedient Servant") stress his total bafflement with Hamilton's bold choices and the people's enthusiasm for them. Hamilton doesn't fathom Burr either, as emphasized in a few lines – he tells him, "I will never understand you" in "The Story of Tonight" (Reprise), and in "Non-Stop," Hamilton protests, "I don't understand how you stand to the side."

In Miranda's telling, they are negative images of each other, Hamilton's heated recklessness contrasting with Burr's icy caution. "Hamilton is this orphan with nothing to lose, and Burr is this orphan with everything to lose," Miranda says. (Mead)

In fact, the historical Burr wanted to become rich and powerful and told his critics, "Great souls have little use for small morals" ("The Duel").

In this first meeting, Hamilton's constant "sir" suggests social conventions less seen today but also his nervousness as he babbles all over himself with constant interjections of "sir," all at awkward beats. He soon establishes that his difficulty is that he's lost control of himself (Hamilton's greatest flaw, presented this early on) and punched the bursar (not a historically accurate event, but a funny one. Also one of the many "Burr" rhymes offered in the show).

Hamilton's untampered babble is more than the show's joke – it was historically true. "I cannot make everyone else as rapid as myself. This you know by experience," he wrote jokingly to his wife (*Papers of Alexander Hamilton*, vol. 22, p. 340). He was also a speedy reader and learner. "Hamilton at once proved himself a student of incomparable energy, racing through his studies with characteristic speed" (Chernow 52).

Burr unhurriedly gives him advice that will return through the show: "Talk less. Smile more…Don't let them know what you're against or what you're for." Thus he establishes himself as the loudmouthed, fast-talking Hamilton's foil and total opposite. Placing the characters side by side is a literary device meant to emphasize their contrast, and also the ideologies they embody. The pair suggest a bold or cautious new America, an optimistic or guarded one. They also mirror many political figures both today and presumably in eras to come. Hamilton tells Burr he is "at your service, sir," a concept that will return. Likewise appearing later is "What will you fall for?"

Ron Chernow has said that Miranda is more sympathetic toward Burr than he was in his book, because he's Hamilton's twin in so many ways (Binelli). In fact, Miranda strongly considered playing the villain in the show, as he did during his first White House performance. He quips, "'Wait for It' and 'The Room Where It Happens' are two of the best songs I've ever written in my life and he got them both" (Browne). As he adds:

> There's enormous fun to playing Burr, which Leslie [Odom, Jr.] finds every night. It's the same thing as, if you're going to be in *Les Mis*, do you want to play Valjean or Javert? Do you want to play the virtuous guy with the crazy high notes who's onstage more? Or do you want to play the badass who's always a step behind him? When I was writing "My Shot," I'd go, "Oh, man, if I could play Hamilton…" And then I would write "Wait for It" and go, "Fuck, if I could play Burr…" I spent a lot of time in both their heads. The reality is, I got to play all the parts. I got to be Angelica and be as smart as her. I got to be Eliza and be as unconditionally loving as her. That's the fun of writing the piece. I got to be Jefferson and basically run out of fucks to give and saunter around my house and try to think of what he would say. (Binelli)

Burr and Hamilton meet with Hamilton in brown (suggesting his humble origins and obscurity) and Burr still in the royal red of boldness and privilege. The color also suggests he's a bringer of destruction, as he will be at the end. Nonetheless, they're fundamentally similar. As the pair meet, Hamilton establishes they're both orphans, both struggling to graduate Princeton in two years. In fact, Burr has succeeded at this, thanks to his connections, while Hamilton is failing. As Miranda adds, "He's Hamilton with privilege! He's Hamilton if Hamilton came from money instead of not" (Binelli). Thus he's who Hamilton might have been, a glimpse of "what if." Like Hamilton, young Burr was abruptly orphaned and sent to live with relatives (his grandparents) who promptly died, then he was shipped off once again. He earned a B.A. by age sixteen, making him also a prodigy, though one with connections and money. Burr is even holding a book, suggesting not just that he's a student but that he shares Hamilton's obsessive love of reading.

Miranda gives Burr sympathetic moments through the show, making him a well-rounded antihero more than a hissing villain. For both characters, he enjoys tracing their diverging paths. He explains:

> When you come from money but have no family, what does that do to you, to your sense of caution? As opposed to Hamilton, who came from nothing and had no family, so, "Fuck it! I might be dead tomorrow, let's go!" And Burr's response to the same set of stimuli – mother died, father died – is "I better not fuck it up. I better not say anything." So it gets at something much more fundamental than politics or political disagreements or personal disagreements. It gets to how we're wired. How do we react to our mortality? Do we shut up and wait for moments to happen, or do we just kind of say whatever we think because who knows what's going to happen? And I think we're all a mix of Hamilton and Burr. I know I am. (Binelli)

Joining the Revolution

After meeting Burr, Hamilton accompanies him to a tavern where he meets Lafayette, Mulligan, and Laurens drunkenly bragging and rapping (historically he didn't meet them all at once, but this is being consolidated for drama). The four burst in with cries of "show time!" that bend the fourth wall a bit: Now that they have come the real show (or perhaps the musical) can start. Their raucous pounding and rapping contrasts with Burr and Hamilton's quiet meeting outside, completely changing the mood to joyous and intrusive in this bastion of male pride.

The tavern buddies are Hamilton in russet brown, Laurens in a deeper chocolate, Mulligan in a sailor's knit cap (or perhaps the street-style hat of a modern rapper) in a dark green coat and Lafayette in navy. Thus they're a spectrum of colors and personalities even beyond considering the racial diversity. It's a good balance between historical and modern. Jack Viertel comments in his book on modern musicals, "From the neck up they look like a motley gang of street-corner revolutionaries in the Bronx in 2015. And they sound like that too" (60).

Each of the revolutionaries introduces himself and his agenda loudly, emphasizing three larger-than-life personalities. The French Lafayette with his heavy accent dreams of "life without a monarchy," yet cannot pronounce English well enough to say "anarchy" (a joke that pays out later when he drops the densest rap lyrics on the show).

Though Hercules Mulligan didn't become a statesman, his name is, as Miranda puts it, "The best rapper moniker I ever heard in my life" so he gets the cool attitude (*Hamilton: The Revolution* 25). In his knit cap, Mulligan frames himself as a talented rapper and a self-taught hero, a tailor's apprentice hoping "to socially advance, instead of sewin' some pants!" He's brash and eager to trash-talk with "Brrrah brraaah! I am Hercules Mulligan/Yes I heard ya mother said 'Come again?'"

The more sincere and idealistic Laurens protests slavery, adding: "But we'll never be truly free/Until those in bondage have the same rights as you and me" and dreams of creating "the first Black battalion." Laurens, though the son of one of South Carolina's most influential planters, with his entire inheritance tied up in slavery, was passionate for abolition and wrote essays hoping to free American slaves to fight in the Revolution. Sadly, his plans were met with derision by the South. Like Hamilton, he was "imbued with a quixotic sense that it was noble to die in a worthy cause" (Chernow 94) and the two adored each other.

31

When asked who "this kid" is who's listening to their own speeches, Hamilton bursts in, introducing himself as "young, scrappy and hungry" in a way they are not. "Unlike the rest of them, he lacks breeding, finesse, a common background. He's an outsider, and he's the one worth watching" (Viertel 59). He raps so passionately for two minutes straight of how, as he puts it, "I am not throwing away my shot" that he commands their attention and leads them in plans for revolution. *Vibe* described the backing as "reminiscent of the '90s" ("Going H.A.M."). The new trio soon join in with his song, dancing along as well.

While making their plans about what each of their "shots" will be, they in fact do shots of alcohol and plot a future until Burr interrupts and warns them, highlighting his own agenda, "You've got to be carefully taught/If you talk, you're gonna get shot!" On this, they all do a shot, giving the word by now a triple meaning. Of course, if this also references the single shot that finally kills Hamilton, we could pile a fourth meaning on top.

Hamilton is the planner who assembles their band, crying: "Let's hatch a plot blacker than the kettle callin' the pot..." and continues fervently rapping until they all stare, stunned. The lights dim. Chastened, he asks, quieter:

> Oh, am I talkin' too loud?
> Sometimes I get over excited, shoot off at the mouth
> I never had a group of friends before
> I promise that I'll make y'all proud.

After a beat, Laurens grins at Hamilton's mouthiness, replying: "Let's get this guy in front of a crowd." Miguel Cervantes, who starred as Hamilton in Chicago in 2016 said: "There's something really refreshing about someone who says what they think [and] who doesn't mince words. Everybody needs to have a friend like that" (Kowalski).

"My Shot" has the revolutionaries planning to "roll like Moses, claimin' our promised land," referencing the conquering of Canaan so they can build God's country. This

32

gives them symbolic moral power – God has blessed their endeavor. Other religious threads will unspool throughout the musical.

The Boston Tea Party happened in December 1773, around the time Hamilton enrolled at university (in fact, Hamilton's first political essay defended the event). The Sons of Liberty met on the Common near King's College on July 6, 1774. There, Hamilton burst into a fiery speech.

> After mounting the platform, the short, boyish speaker started out haltingly, then caught fire in a burst of oratory. If true to his later style, Hamilton gained energy as he spoke. He endorsed the Boston Tea Party, deplored the closure of Boston's port, endorsed colonial unity against unfair taxation, and came down foursquare for a boycott of British goods. (Chernow 55)

The crowd, stared, stunned, then burst into a standing ovation. "From that moment on, he was treated as a youthful hero of the cause" (Chernow 55). Parliament was unwilling to extend the rights of British free men to Americans, something that angered the colonists to the point of war, though they weren't yet certain independence was their goal.

Onstage, the other tavern patrons sing and dance with Hamilton, and the scene opens to the streets of New York and lit up scaffolding, with even more eager listeners, emphasizing how the word is spreading wider and wider.

Laurens goes around telling everyone they must "rise up." A ring of light fills the stage, and the turntable in the floor spins, emphasizing travels through the entire city as well as a world revolving into something new. The gang fetch Hamilton a soapbox and he hesitates (while the other actors freeze) then steps up to the box as his rapping thoughts transition to his speech.

The staging here sparkles with drama. The light around the soapbox briefly resembles either a spotlight or target. After his speech, everyone bursts from tight circle around him like they've actually been shot from a cannon.

Then he's dancing with crowd even as Hercules Mulligan enters with a dramatic leap. Golden light makes them seem colored like multiracial New Yorkers, not bland ghosts this time. Dramatic moves fills the stage, so energetic and acrobatic they're warlike. Hamilton dances with hand over his heart, and the crowd mirrors him, emphasizing they act as an extension of him as he develops his patriotism. When the crowd raise their arms, they seem to cheer him. Hamilton soon switches from singing with the crowd to rapping on his own, emphasizing how he'll break convention and stand out as an individual. Together they sing "Rise up!" (another ongoing motif). The new revolutionaries (minus Burr who's more hesitant) march forward in middle of it all. Hamilton ends powerfully, with arm thrust into the air like the show's logo.

Historically, Hamilton joined the Revolution around this time. With the British preparing an assault on New York, he formed an artillery company with some fellow students including Hercules Mulligan and seized cannon and rifles from a British armory. The oldest unit in the American Army today is Hamilton's unit – the first battalion, fifth field artillery. "Hamilton betrayed none of the novice's typical air of slipshod indecision and made a profound impression on several senior military figures, who joined his swelling circle of admirers" (Chernow 73). In one skirmish with the British, Hamilton was said to have fired a canon at them, slicing through a portrait of King George II in the chapel (Chernow 85).

One night a mob gathered, seeking the British sympathizer and college head Myles Cooper. Officer Stephen Colden wrote:

> Dr. Cooper's a Tory and an obnoxious man. The mob breaks down the gates of the college and is gathering on the steps with tar and feathers, yelling, "prepare for your doom!" Then I see an amazing scene. A student comes out on the stoop, all by himself, and begins arguing with the

Risking his own life, Hamilton lectured the mob on the importance of an honorable revolution until Cooper could climb over the back fence and escape with his life. Thus Hamilton showed how the revolution was won mattered as much to him as the cause itself. He also demonstrated his amazing gift for language.

The next short song, "The Story of Tonight," moves indoors to chairs for a quieter number, bringing the story back to the small band of friends. The innocence in the sweet melody comes from the fact that Miranda actually wrote it at age sixteen, emphasizing the group's young romanticism and belief that they can win without suffering and dying (Miranda and McCarter, *Hamilton: The Revolution* 35). "This is the tune of brotherhood among these friends, but it can also encapsulate rowdiness and the lewd roast that occurs [after the wedding]," Miranda notes (*Hamilton: The Revolution* 86). "Raise a glass to the four of us / Tomorrow there'll be more of us" emphasizes the contrast between masses of revolutionaries outside and four quiet planners inside – a public versus private motif that will extend through the show.

The chorus of "They'll tell the story of tonight" likewise bends the fourth wall, as this is a contribution to history as well as this musical. Further, it echoes the vital concept of who is telling the story.

Soon after, Samuel Seabury arrives in clergy robes to sing in a churchlike conventional ballad, "Heed not the rabble who scream revolution / They have not your interests at heart." "Farmer Refuted" is sing-song, preachy, and likely the slowest song in the whole production. It's repetitive and Seabury even appears to be reading his sermon onstage. He's the voice of traditionalism.

Mulligan the hip rabble-rouser tells Hamilton without missing a beat, "Oh my God. Tear this dude apart." This Hamilton does, even "using the same vowels and cadences and talking over him," as Miranda puts it. This is his particular impressive "superpower" (*Hamilton: The Revolution* 49). Seabury stands on his podium while Hamilton darts around him criticizing his language, active and cheeky.

On a basic level, the American Revolution was driven by words: fiery statements of principle; charges of imperialist oppression; accusations of betrayal; fine points of governance; even wordy obfuscations to gloss over disagreements that could have sabotaged the country at its start. What better musical genre to tell this tale? (Tommasini and Caramanica)

Historically, the Sons of Liberty had burned Seabury's loyalist essay by "A Westchester Farmer" amid much derision. They even went so far as to tar and feather the copies. Hamilton anonymously published "A Full Vindication of the Measures of the Congress" in response to Seabury's words, and Seabury then rebutted it. Hamilton shot back with "The Farmer Refuted," an eighty-page essay published in 1775. "I am neither merchant, nor farmer," he wrote. "I address you because I wish well to my country" (*Papers of Alexander Hamilton*, vol 1, 65). Hamilton called Seabury's answer "puerile and fallacious" and added, "I will venture to pronounce it one of the most ludicrous performances which has been exhibited to public view during all the present controversy" (*Papers of Alexander Hamilton*, vol. 1, 82). Seabury was finally cowed.

It's understandable that their letter writing campaign should be updated to public speeches. Chernow even called "The Farmer Refuted" "a bravura performance," a phrase that may have caught Miranda's imagination (61). Thus onstage the pair aren't battling with letters but by preaching to the crowd and struggling to outsing the other. Hamilton's arguments are more complexly rhymed and much more spontaneous. Hamilton is the new way, stomping out the old. Then with a "Silence!" from the guards, the king interrupts both their arguments and presents his own song. This provides a fine segue into the true voice of the royalist movement – the king himself.

King George III

Miranda describes having a drink with British actor Hugh Laurie from *House* and wondering what the king's response to the Revolution would be. Laurie promptly replied, "You'll be back!" (*Hamilton: The Revolution* 57). All this made it into the show, offering more contrast between the colonies and Merrie Old England.

The king appears pompously alone when he sings, in contrast with the brotherly Founding Fathers. He's the only main character played by a white actor, with iconic ermine and gold royal robes and a large crown. This is also one of the most "traditional musical theatre" numbers. He thus seems to embody the old world of rules and royal commands – all the Founding Fathers are rejecting to tell a new story.

He stands regally (perhaps unable to move under the weight of all the clothes) and doesn't dance. In fact, propping himself on his scepter makes him look especially impotent in the force of the Revolution. Nonetheless, his skepticism of the rebellion emphasizes that while Americans know it will triumph, those at the time had no idea – no colonies had ever successfully revolted or demanded rule by consent of the governed.

"In the show's funniest bit, King George III sings British Invasion pop, a breakup tune addressed to the United States…that blatantly draws on the Beatles" (Hiatt). This British invasion certainly makes a clear pun. As it blends Beatles tunes, the "Getting Better" guitar appears on the outro and the tune echoes "With a Little Help From My Friends." Musical director Alex Lacamoire adds:

> There's a "Penny Lane" reference in the vibe. In the first chorus, the vibes go, [*hums "Penny Lane" chords*]. There's a "Mr. Kite" reference: At "You say your love is draining and you can't go on," the synth goes, *bah dunna-nah, dunna-*

> *nah, dunna-nah.* The bass line is a total Paul-ism. At "My
> sweet submissive subject," the bass does *da-dunnoo-
> dunnoo*, the high triplet fill, and the bass is muted so it
> sounds like a Hofner. The drums — *a-ts-ts-ts-ts, ta-ts-ts* —
> are a fill I know I stole from Ringo. And the way [Jonathan]
> Groff intones, "Everybody!" at the end is a little like Lennon
> in "All You Need Is Love." That idea came up in the studio
> last minute. (Jones)

The ensemble (and generally the audience) joins King George
here, only adding to the goofiness. Of course, they stand still
and poised, then bow – they are courtiers paid to sing along –
not crowds won over by great speeches. His songs are silly to
the point of self-parody as he gleefully sings "da da da da da"
in Beatles style but to entertain only himself. He also sings,
"When you're gone/I'll go mad/So don't throw away this
thing we had," referencing his famous madness.

The pompous purple light that circles him towards the
end of the number nods to the color scheme of entitled
Jefferson of Act II. There's clever play on the word subject
and many break-up puns. In fact, his "You'll be Back" theme
emphasizes his role as jilted lover in the new America that's
left him behind. It's also ridiculously wrong since obviously
America never returned to English rule or even tried to. The
lyrics become even more ludicrous when he decides that
"when push/Comes to shove" he will "send a fully armed
battalion" and "kill your friends and family/To remind you of
my love."

Just after "Yorktown" he returns, undercutting their
triumph with the question of "What Comes Next?" As the
war ends, there's a sudden mood shift from serious to silly.
George stamps his foot, sulks, and quips "awesome, wow,"
with pouring sarcasm. The audience cracks up. He's lost the
robe, so in his short breeches, he has echoes of a naughty
child. When "I'm so blue" turns his spotlight blue, he also
opens the fourth wall again, reminding spectators they're
watching a play. However, hidden in his ridiculousness are
some logical questions: "What comes next?/You've been

WHO TELLS YOUR STORY?

freed/Do you know how hard it is to lead?" As he concludes, they're on their own. Of course, this somber conclusion is undercut by his flipping up his hands dismissively as he strides off.

His third number "I Know Him" has the king express astonishment that Washington has stepped down, clearly a jarring shocker for many born to power: "I wasn't aware that was something a person could do," he says, bewildered, emphasizing his own lack of greatness. With his usual juvenile smirking, he adds, "They will tear each other into pieces/Jesus Christ, this will be fun!" He concludes, "President John Adams, good luck," implying nothing of the sort, and then finally plonks himself in a chair onstage and watches the political show to follow, his role as outsider commentator complete. (Though he does dance in time with the next song and with the Reynolds Pamphlet scandal, to the audience's delight.) As he watches the musical, the fourth wall wobbles once more.

His "oceans rise, empires fall" appears in all three songs as a chorus, stressing how the king is barely affected by this rebellion. Even his tune never varies, nor does his message. While the heroes grow and change, he remains a static motionless pillar, much like a royal painting.

His presence is yet another contrast, reminding the revolutionaries there are consequences to their choices but mostly providing sarcastic commentary from an outsider's perspective. No longer responsible for the colonies, he can reflect on all the mistakes they're making and point out all they've abandoned, even as they charge ahead.

Fighting the War

After the king's cheerful number, the crowd sing despondently on a watery stage about how surrounded they are. The Schuyler Sisters stand in front, giving the crowd a face.

Washington actually gets more of a buildup than the king,

and as the two Georges are introduced back to back, everything about their demeanor and movement, as well as their musical choices, polarize. For his entrance, Washington strides confidently onstage. His hand rests on his sword. His words pound, so much so that this is more rhyming-on-beat than singing. In "Right Hand Man," he "raps commandingly over a grimy, bass-heavy hip-hop beat and ascends to soaring R&B ballads" (Mead). Hard syllables dictate his rap, practically a yell:

> We are outgunned
> Outmanned
> Outnumbered
> Outplanned
> We gotta make an all-out stand
> Ayo, I'm gonna need a right-hand man.

Daveed Diggs (Lafayette) notes that "Washington raps in this very metronomic way because that is similar to how he thinks" (*Hamilton's America*). As Washington narrates the battle, the ensemble's punctuating "boom," each time setting off leaps and jolts, suggests a barrage of fire rather than the intricate dance of war. Dire straits clearly threaten them.

Washington immediately requests to let down his guard and "tell the people how I feel a second," emphasizing his lack of the king's artifice and pageantry. Blue light glazes Washington's monologue, in contrast with the king's red-purple. The blue suggests the British naval invasion and Washington's despair as they plunge into a devastating sea battle and lose.

Emphasizing a new role for him, Burr promptly dresses Hamilton in an officer's coat. Clearly, Burr is still a mentor here, until he can hand Hamilton off to the new general. In a touch of humility and practicality, Washington wears the same blue military uniform as the other rebels, only decorated with epaulettes, a sash, and his famous tricorn. Under the rebels' blue coat, Lafayette adds lots of gold trim and shining epaulettes too, suggesting his own lack of modesty.

General Washington suffered a humiliating defeat in the battle and was forced to abandon New York City. By this point Hamilton had come to the attention of three other generals – Alexander McDougall, Nathanael Greene, and Lord Stirling (Chernow 85). Hamilton and his artillery company joined Washington's army and held off the advancing British in what is now Harlem. Jimmy Napoli, Hamilton Tour Guide, explains:

> The first time George Washington sees Hamilton, he's putting together an earthwork. While the rest of the Continental Army is crying, weeping over what happened in Brooklyn, Hamilton is organizing and getting things together. That evening, Washington actually invites him to dine with him in his tent and speaks with him. (*Alexander Hamilton: American Experience*)

He and Burr see Washington at the same time in the musical – as Washington rejects the smarmy Burr and chooses more genuine, eager Hamilton, the pair resemble brothers squabbling for their father's love…and only one is chosen. Hamilton became, very early in the Revolution, Washington's adopted son and, more officially, an aide-de-camp at age twenty-two.

> The two men had complementary talents, values, and opinions that survived many strains over their twenty-two years together. Washington possessed the outstanding judgement, sterling character, and clear sense of purpose needed to guide his somewhat wayward protégé; he saw that the wayward Hamilton needed a steadying hand. Hamilton, in turn, contributed philosophical depth, administrative expertise, and comprehensive policy knowledge that nobody in Washington's camp ever matched. (Chernow 88)

Washington gives Hamilton a pen (not a sword or rifle)…a tool he will use for the rest of the story. As Hamilton takes the position, the light turns a more hopeful purple as Hamilton, businesslike, raps about all he can organize. He recruits his friends, sends out spies, and adds, "I'll write to Congress and tell 'em we need supplies, you rally the guys, master the element of surprise." General and aide stand side by side in an identically-dressed partnership. Historian Willard Sterne Randall explains:

> Washington had all sorts of brave soldiers, and even some experienced officers. But what he didn't have was anybody who could write as copiously as Hamilton could. Washington's best writing and correspondence is not Washington at all – it's Alexander Hamilton, from the time he's twenty-one years old. (*Alexander Hamilton: American Experience*)

The musical stresses Hamilton's frustration as he longs for the glory of battle. Meanwhile, Washington acts as the older mentor and urges caution. His character comes off as the wise and aloof Father of our Country, less deconstructed and flawed than the others.

In the spring of 1776, Burr joined George Washington's staff in Manhattan. However, he quit within two weeks, wanting to be on the battlefield over the "insular world of the commander's staff," according to historian Nancy Isenberg (33). He served under General Israel Putnam and saved an entire brigade from capture... including Hamilton. To Burr's misery, Washington failed to commend Burr's actions in the next day's General Orders (the fastest way to obtain a promotion in rank) (Lomask 82). This added to Burr's sense of unfairness at the world.

The Schuyler Sisters

Peggy, Angelica and Eliza enter New York in peach, yellow, and seafoam Colonial dresses. Angelica's dress is the most elaborate and Peggy's is the simplest, reflecting their personalities and roles in the story. Eliza's soft green shows her as a nurturer happy to tend her garden. (Also, as Hamilton dons green to deal with politics and money, they become a matched set as perfect couple.) Peggy's yellow is youthful, innocent, untried. Eliza's peach is more sensual. Each also has a musical motif attached to her name, repeated whenever the name is used.

In crowd scenes like the song "Alexander Hamilton" they wear three shades of off white, differentiating them as a trio in their long skirts but also blending them in with the crowd. "Me? I loved him" all three announce in the introductory number. The use of "I" not "we" makes this personal – each loved him in a different way. Since Peggy later plays Maria, she brings in the forbidden affair as well as the innocent love of the sister-in-law.

Eliza is the caretaker who fills in for Alexander's mother and tells her part of the exposition in the first number:

> When he was ten his father split, full of it, debt-ridden
> Two years later, see Alex and his mother bed-ridden
> Half-dead sittin in their own sick, the scent thick

Thus she replaces the maternal figure in Hamilton's life and becomes a source of trustworthy support. The team wanted Philippa Soo, who could make Eliza's goodness compelling, as soon as they discovered her in the stage adaptation of *War and Peace: Natasha, Pieree, and the Great Comet of 1812* (Miranda and McCarter, *Hamilton: The Revolution* 107).

As they sing "Look around, look around" in "The Schuyler Sisters" they alternately dance with the crowd or stand as a trio, holding hands, twirling in a star, or forming a triangle with Angelica in front. Burr accuses them of slumming, and since everyone around them is working but they're strutting in fine dresses, the accusation seems valid. Their chorus, "Look around, look around at how/Lucky we are to be alive right now!" emphasizes their cheerfulness but also their political awareness of the coming revolution.

The song sets their personalities in contrast as Peggy fearfully sings "Daddy said not to go downtown." The other sisters dismiss her worries. Meanwhile, Angelica is the leader, standing in the middle of their triangle and singing the more adventurous section of the tune. She's also taking the aggressive lines and showing political awareness as she raps:

> I've been reading *Common Sense* by Thomas Paine
> So men say that I'm intense or I'm insane
> You want a revolution? I want a revelation
> So listen to my declaration:

She wants to be equal with men, something as anachronistic as her bragging about her intensity. This is traditionally only a role for great male revolutionaries. Nonetheless, Miranda gives her the voice of a defiant feminist, updating her daring personality along with the revolutionary rappers.

Her dramatic gestures, backed up by her sisters, make them appear a polished singing group – in fact, the trio sound like the R&B group Destiny's Child.

> Musical director Alex Lacamoire explained that the song originally had a throwback Daft Punk/Pharrell feel, but after viewing a series of Vines with the three actresses improving on Destiny's Child songs, he reworked the song to give it a Destiny's Child vibe, then let the sisters add their own harmonies to the tune; he "realized there's nothing in the song as cool as the harmonies the girls do when they're fucking around, so we...just let them riff" (Jones)

Soon enough, the hero meets the trio. "Hamilton was girl crazy and brimming with libido. Throughout his career, at unlikely moments, he tended to grow flirtatious, even giddy, with women" (Chernow 93). As historian Joanne B. Freeman explains:

> Hamilton's a person who liked to conquer all situations. And if he was in a room of men, he'd want to win every argument. And if he's in a room of women and men, he wants to win every woman as well. And I think he likes to just be the guy who wins, you know – the best, the first, the top of the heap. (*Alexander Hamilton: American Experience*)

At an officers' ball, he indeed was enchanted with the fetching Eliza and began courting her. Phillipa Soo (Eliza), tells that she had to figure out her relationship to Hamilton and answer questions like, "Who is this man to me, and why do I love him?"

> In the end, she realized her "research was already here for me. It became less about finding facts about Eliza and Alexander Hamilton and more about just watching Lin. I remember him coming into the rehearsal room in his slippers, because he'd been across the street writing. And I was like, 'Oh, my God, this guy is nonstop!' Kind of like Hamilton." (Binelli)

In fact, Eliza spoke proudly of her husband's "Elasticity of mind. Variety of his knowledge. Playfulness of his wit. Excellence of his heart. His immense forbearance [and] virtues" (qtd. in Chernow 132).

Meanwhile, Hamilton had already imagined an ideal wife, with qualities Eliza fit:

> She must be young, good looking, shapely – I'm very insistent on a good shape. Sensible, well bred, but not someone who puts on airs. Chaste and tender. As for money, well, it seems to be an essential ingredient to happiness in this world, and as I don't have any now and am not likely to get much of my own, I hope my wife will bring at least enough to take care of her own luxuries. It doesn't matter what her politics are, I have arguments enough to convert her to my views. (*Alexander Hamilton: American Experience*)

In "Helpless," Eliza sings in the middle of the ball as the dancers whirl around her on the turntable, lit in pink. Though she's the architect of the scene, the fact that her world is spinning suggests love but also literal helplessness – she cannot woo the man for herself. Her green ballgown suggests total innocence. In fact, Eliza is so shy she must send her livelier sister to bring Hamilton over. Historically, Eliza was "the most self-effacing 'founding mother,' doing everything in her power to focus the spotlight exclusively on her husband" (Chernow 130). She explains in "Helpless":

> I have never been the type to try and grab the spotlight
> We were at a revel with some rebels on a hot night
> Laughin' at my sister as she's dazzling the room
> Then you walked in and my heart went "Boom!"

The lyric "My heart went boom" (complete with light flash on the final word) is a gentler reflection of cannons, emphasizing the war is still going on outside.

"Helpless" has a strong Beyoncé vibe. For its origins, Miranda recalls nineties pop/hip-hop crossovers including Mary J. Blige and Method Man's "I'll Be There for You/You're All I Need to Get By" and Beyoncé's "Crazy in Love" with a guest verse from Jay Z (*Hamilton: The Revolution* 68). Lacamoire explains, "The Beyoncé reference is 'Stressin'! Blessin'!' sounds like 'Houston rocket!' [in 'Countdown']. We asked the girls to deliver it like that" (Jones). There's also Cole Porter and Ja Rule in this sweet Pop/R&B tune that blends banter and exposition. The gentlemen spin their ladies then slide on the floor, offering a hybrid breakdance rather than one that's modern or traditional.

Eliza is innocent here but not brainless – she knows her love is true after reading Hamilton's letters, not just because of their attraction and classic musical-style meeting. In fact, it's the "across the ballroom their eyes met" scene...except that Hamilton is flirting in the corner with Angelica. There's clear jealousy mixed with the romance as Eliza adds, "She grabbed you by the arm, I'm thinkin' 'I'm through.'" Hamilton, in turn, seems to think this moment is about him and Angelica:

> HAMILTON: Where are you taking me?
> ANGELICA: I'm about to change your life
> HAMILTON: Then by all means, lead the way

Angelica introduces him to Eliza, and Hamilton quickly turns gallant, telling her, "If it takes fighting a war for us to meet, it will have been worth it."

Angelica leaves them and the match is made. As Hamilton wrote to Laurens:

> Have you not heard that I am on the point of becoming a benedict [a newly engaged or married man who had long been a bachelor]? I confess my sins. I am guilty. Next fall completes my doom. I give up my liberty to Miss Schuyler. She is a good hearted girl who I am sure will never play the termagant; though not a genius she has good sense enough to be agreeable, and though not a beauty, she has fine black eyes – is rather handsome and has every other requisite of the exterior to make a lover happy. And believe me, I am lover in earnest, though I do not speak of the perfections of my Mistress in the enthusiasm of Chivalry. (*Papers of Alexander Hamilton*, vol. 2, p. 347-348).

However, Angelica adds to her sister later, "I'm just sayin', if you really loved me, you would share him" (a historical quip in her letters that graces this love triangle in the show). This suggestion is provocative, rule-breaking and humorous like Angelica herself, but also suggests where the messy relationship will go. Two weeks later, Hamilton gains permission to wed Eliza. He tells her, contradictingly:

> Your family brings out a different side of me
> Peggy confides in me, Angelica tried to take a bite of me
> No stress, my love for you is never in doubt
> We'll get a little place in Harlem and we'll figure it out

Eliza is surprised at this frank confession of Angelica's apparent move on her fiancé, but the wedding goes ahead. There's a swirl of letters being sent and delivered which feels like more of the joyful ball choreography, swirling into the wedding as her sisters veil Eliza. The courtship and wedding are both balls with the swirling turntable, couple's letters, and flashback adding to the ever-spinning blur.

On December 14, 1780, Hamilton, at age 25, wed

Elizabeth, who was 23 (Chernow 148).

However, as Angelica gives the wedding toast, the world swirls around her as the cast chant "rewind," undoing the music and the actions to flash back to the original ball. This convention is basically unseen in musicals (which more often do parallel scenes side by side) though these flashbacks that change the nature of the present are popular in television and film – another burst of modernity into the musical form.

Her memories are lit in the blue of memory instead of Eliza's dreamy pink. Angelica and Hamilton meet and he instantly provokes her with the words of "Satisfied":

> HAMILTON: You strike me as a woman who has never been satisfied.
> ANGELICA: I'm sure I don't know what you mean. You forget yourself.
> HAMILTON: You're like me. I'm never satisfied.

If Eliza was "Helpless" Angelica wants to be "Satisfied" – on *Twitter*, Miranda quoted the real letter from Angelica to Hamilton that inspired the song's lyrics: "You are happy my dear friend to find consolation in 'words & thoughts.' I cannot be so easily satisfied" (Eggert).

Miranda adds, "There is all manner of satisfaction – sexual, emotional, financial. It's also a code word used in dueling – 'to demand satisfaction'" (*Hamilton: The Revolution* 80). There's a sexual suggestion here but also one of having all she wants or of being a social climber who's as ambitious and clever as Hamilton. The two are mentally attuned – Angelica thinks, "So this is what it feels like to match wits/ With someone at your level!" Nonetheless, she "gives" him to Eliza – this is sisterly love but also Angelica's ambition for a rich man of social status. As she puts it:

> I'm a girl in a world in which
> My only job is to marry rich
> My father has no sons so I'm the one
> Who has to social climb for one

At the time this choice would determine a woman's entire future and often the status of her family as well. Angelica is behaving wisely for her era, as her more romantic sister hurls herself into marriage with a penniless, nameless man (though granted, the historical Angelica actually had several brothers and was married when she met Hamilton).

Angelica's frantically bursting rap during this scene emphasizes how quickly her mind works, and how many thoughts she has between each line of dialogue. The speed was meant to show her brilliance and racing thoughts, not as a way of showing off. "She's demonstrating that Angelica read Hamilton the moment she saw him, but it didn't stop her from falling in love with him and didn't stop her calculating *in a moment* to yield to her sister's love for him." (*Hamilton: The Revolution* 79). Miranda adds:

> The lyrics to "Satisfied" – in which Angelica Schuyler recounts how Hamilton and her sister Eliza met and married – are some of the most intricate I've ever written. I can't even rap them, but Renee Elise Goldsberry, who plays Angelica – that's her conversational speed. That's how fast she thinks. You really get the sense that Angelica's the smartest person in the room, and she reads Hamilton within a moment of meeting him. (DiGiacomo)

Once again, she shares much with Hamilton. Of course, there's one striking difference which reveals itself through the story – Angelica, with her tight sisterhood, puts her sister before herself. Alexander, an orphan, loves Eliza but doesn't prioritize her needs over his for years, because he was never taught how to be a family man.

Miranda describes having a moment with a girl whom his best friend then marries. Still, both remember the flirtation that can't be unsaid (*Hamilton: The Revolution* 167). Of course, as Angelica comments, she will get to keep Hamilton in her life and they're forever bound. Publically, she smiles and toasts them, whatever she feels within. Historically, she remained very close to her sister and her sister's husband, conveying love for both in every letter. Chernow calls the relationship between the trio a "curious ménage a trois" and adds that, unusually, the women's "shared love for Hamilton seemed to deepen their sisterly bond" (Chernow 134). Their friendship was "so potent and obvious that many people assumed they were lovers. At the very least, theirs was a friendship of unusual ardor" (Chernow 133). Miranda describes it as an emotional affair, whether or not there was a physical one. Renée Elise Goldsberry adds, "It feels wrong but it's also necessary and crucial for her existence. He gives her something that she gets nowhere else, and she has to have it" (Miranda and McCarter, *Hamilton: The Revolution* 167). At the same time, both are devoted to Eliza. "The love affair is really Eliza and loving him through her" Goldsberry concludes (Miranda and McCarter, *Hamilton: The Revolution* 167).

In Angelica's cut second act song, "Congratulations," she touches more specifically on her and Hamilton's unrequited love and addresses the chance of their having an affair (Dreamcatcher). As she points out that his letters were all that sustained her through her loveless marriage, she floats the idea that now that she's come back to New York they might finally have been able to consummate the relationship or at least be closer…but now she's taking Eliza's side instead. Leaving this song out makes their relationship more ambiguous in the show – a better reflection of history.

Eliza's story follows with Hamilton angry when she summons him home because she's pregnant. Nonetheless, she struggles to soothe him and remind him of all he should be grateful for. A guitar and piano support her words with a sweet melody. Of course, Eliza's no doormat, as she makes Washington send Hamilton home and matches wits with one of the foremost Congressional debaters through the show.

When she greets him with her signature optimistic "Look around, look around at how lucky we are/To be alive right now," she's standing by the stone bench signifying the exterior of their house. It's gravelike, foreshadowing several

events to come. She wears grey and the light is blue-purple –
the gloom of twilight instead of the pink of love or gold of
eagerness. Thus there's more than a touch of melancholy.
"I don't pretend to know/The challenges you're
facing/The worlds you keep erasing and creating in your
mind," she sings, emphasizing the gap in understanding.
Creating another gap, she returns to her refrain "That would
be enough" – she is satisfied but he cannot be. He soon
leaves her once more.

Burr Returns

In "The Story of Tonight" (Reprise), Hamilton is
drinking with his friends at the wedding's end. Hamilton and
Burr inspire each other as foils – each wants what the other
has – a command versus the general's respect. "Congrats to
you, Lieutenant Colonel/I wish I had your command instead
of manning George's journal," Hamilton quips. Meanwhile,
cautious Burr is having a secret affair with a British officer's
wife while Hamilton has celebrated a respectable public
marriage. Each gives the other a well-meaning piece of advice
(enjoy your life/seize what you want). Each dismisses it.

Burr and Hamilton compete through the story, seeking
the same jobs and the same friends, from the law offices to
the capital. They both charm plenty of women. Burr even is
attracted to one of Hamilton's loves – in "The Schuyler
Sisters" Burr and Angelica fall into a flirtation of a sort:

> ANGELICA: Burr, you disgust me
> BURR: Ah, so you've discussed me
> I'm a trust fund, baby, you can trust me!

Like Washington, Angelica has no use for Burr, only
Hamilton.

Historically, Burr was raised with stern Puritanical views.
All his family were reverends. In fact, Burr was the grandson
of Jonathan Edwards, who wrote the threatening Puritan

sermon "Sinners in the Hands of an Angry God." As his grandfather thundered:

> You that are young men and women have an extraordinary opportunity - but if you neglect it, it will be with you as it is with those that spend away all the precious days of youth in sin! Let everyone fly out of Sodom! Haste and escape for your lives! ("The Duel")

When he grew older, Aaron Burr rebelled against his strict upbringing and rejected all this enforced morality. He spent all his time drinking and flirting…in fact, several women claimed he'd gotten them pregnant, and he flippantly commented, "When a woman does me the honor to name me the father of her child, I shall always be too gallant to decline the honor" ("The Duel"). His love for the married Theodosia was just one indiscretion of many.

In "Wait For It," Burr sings a poignant song about the kinds of justice he's found – love or death "doesn't discriminate/Between the sinners/And the saints." He loses those he loves and is having an imperfect relationship, but he will continue doing what he does best, "Wait for it." Of course, some of his specific denials seem suspiciously defensive: "I'm not falling behind or running late…I'm not standing still/I am lying in wait." As he protests overmuch, it sounds as if he is in fact falling behind and standing still, a concept he complains about later.

Miranda explains, "Hamilton's response to loss is to go as fast as he can. Burr's response to loss is 'I'm not going to do anything until I know it's the right move. I'm alive. Other people I know are dead. There's a reason for that" (*Hamilton's America*). As he adds:

> "I feel like I have been Burr in my life as many times as I have been Hamilton. I think we've all had moments where we've seen friends and colleagues zoom past us, either to success, or to marriage, or to homeownership, while we lingered where we were – broke, single, jobless. And you tell yourself, 'Wait for it.'" (Mead)

Succumbing to his upbringing, Burr grows more directly religious, as "Wait for It" spends the entire song comparing "the sinners and the saints." This obliquely references Matthew 5:44-45:

> But I tell you, love your enemies and pray for those who persecute you, that you may be children of your Father in heaven. He causes his sun to rise on the evil and the good, and sends rain on the righteous and the unrighteous.

The "takes and it takes and it takes" line plays with Job 1:21, in which the beleaguered Job says, "Naked I came from my mother's womb, and naked I will depart. The Lord gave and the Lord has taken away."

Thus though Burr tries to be as selfless and righteous as Matthew (of "turn the other cheek"), he feels like Job – a righteous man who is unfairly persecuted by forces greater than himself. As his lyrics add: "My grandfather was a fire and brimstone preacher/but there are things that the homilies and hymns won't teach ya." With this quote, Burr struggles with traditional religion – being devout and following his grandfather's teachings hasn't helped him, any more than his own political strategies have. As he faces the fact that sinners and saints both suffer, he teeters on the edge of despair as well as turning to malice. His comment in narration about Hamilton "being seated at the right hand of the father" casts Hamilton as the beloved son, Jesus, while Burr is his spiteful rival, Judas.

The song emphasizes how he's tugged in opposing directions. Lacamoire explains:

> "Wait for It" is my favorite track on the record. I love that the beginning is so contained, and then all of a sudden the bridge just goes *BWAAAH!* and it's got that epic feel. In that moment, Burr feels like a lion hiding in the bushes. What I love about it on the record is that we took big chances in terms of how it's panned. Especially at the end, there's a lot of left and right happening — the guys on the left, the girls on the right: "Wait for it!" "Wait for it!" It oscillates between

your ears, almost like the voices in Burr's head, every angle singing to him what his mantra is. (Jones)

Unlike the crowd dance of "My Shot," the chorus here that support Burr are firmly planted in their chairs. Their repeated refrains almost mock him. In four corners they box Burr in while a dramatic blue light on him shows his sadness. The chorus are lit in the gold of ambition but Burr cannot reach them – he sings alone in the dark, emphasizing how lost he is.

> My mother was a genius
> My father commanded respect
> When they died they left no instructions
> Just a legacy to protect

With his abandonment by those who were meant to guide him, the audience roots for Burr. At the same time, he's frustrated that Hamilton is more beloved than himself. "I am the one thing in life I can control," he finally, tragically concludes.

On playing Burr, his actor Leslie Odom, Jr., says, "Lin is asking you to bring your complete and total self to the stage – all your joy, all your rage, all your pain, your capacity for fun." Because of this Burr is "arguably the best role for a male actor of color in the musical theater canon" (Miranda and McCarter, *Hamilton: The Revolution* 90). He adds that he sings it differently each night as the audience changes.

After the war, his "Dear Theodosia" humanizes him even more. "When you came into the world, you cried and it broke my heart," he sings to his baby. In his red waistcoat and shirt sleeves, he's more domestic and vulnerable than in his streetwear.

Hamilton too has a child and each tries to express his love and make the world a better place, as both observe, "My father wasn't around." They sing in chairs side by side in identical squares of light that suggest nursery windows. (The box shapes suggest responsibility and permanence as well.)

54

For an instant, they share the same life experience and respond the same way…then Hamilton is appointed Secretary of the Treasury and their paths diverge as Burr remains unhappily behind. The moment of connection has passed.

Yorktown

Hamilton pleads with Washington for active duty. But the General refuses to let his valuable secretary go. He sits writing in a single spotlight as the army bustles around him. Like Burr has been many times, Hamilton is now narrator. Meanwhile, the Army starves for supplies. In Washington's name, Hamilton is barraging Congress with requests for boots, blankets and food. Congress only responds by holding debates and forming committees. "Local merchants deny us equipment, assistance/They only take British money, so sing a song of sixpence," Hamilton complains in "Stay Alive." Historian Joanne B. Freeman adds:

> This makes him crazy. Even in this dire moment, Congress can't act in a coordinated, in a centralized manner? There's something seriously wrong here. So the war is a concrete lesson in what, to him, feels like the humiliation of a weak and powerless national government. (*Alexander Hamilton: American Experience*)

In the midst of this, a newly-promoted Charles Lee blunders horribly. When enough people have died, then Lee disparages Washington, Laurens challenges Lee. Ironically, Hamilton advises him, "Do not throw away your shot" – meaning his political career. This makes sense in context, but Hamilton will spend the next two duels resolving that he and his son should literally throw away their shots. As the same actor plays Laurens and Philip, there's a fascinating flip here.

The turntable emphasizes events spiraling out of control again while the rings of lights suggest a disturbing bullseye. The duel ensues, with Hamilton and Burr as seconds. Historically, this was Hamilton's first duel. "Always insecure about his status in the world, Hamilton was a natural adherent to dueling, with its patrician overtones. Lacking a fortune or family connections, he guarded his reputation jealously" (Chernow 117). Hamilton also gets in a crack about hoping that "heaven or hell" will take you – emphasizing his flippancy about the religion that so tortures Burr. The two men with their opposing viewpoints face off. Of course, as Burr protests that duels are "dumb and immature" but Hamilton replies that some matters of honor are worth it, they contrast again and foreshadow the final duel that awaits.

The "10 Duel Commandments" (with religious implications in this phrasing) explain the orderly, well-defined rules of the duel, an honorable, socially acceptable practice. This scene sets up how duels work, preparing the audience for the more significant ones of the second act, where the song gets a reprise. The code duello allowed a man to defend his dignity and honor, showing he was brave enough to back up his words with his life. One version, throwing away one's shot, let the men show mercy as well as courage.

The song is specifically modeled after "The Ten Crack Commandments," Christopher Wallace's guide to selling drugs. Miranda comments, "It's a song about illegal activity, and how it works. And we're both stealing the structure from Moses" (Mead). With a bang, the duel concludes, Washington sends Hamilton home, and Hamilton fears his shot is gone.

His home is only a step away when he agrees to go, symbolizing how the only thing parting him and his wife is himself. For the first time since the wedding, Eliza speaks up, reminding Hamilton "how lucky we are" without fame or fortune. However, there is a disconnect – her pregnancy, which makes her urge Hamilton towards domesticity, only pressures him to become a war hero and seize the advancement this can bring him.

Historically, Hamilton resigned as aide de camp, and threatened to quit the army. Washington finally relented and gave him a battalion in 1781.

In the show it's the "secret weapon" – fast rapping,

joyously controlled Lafayette who dictates what Washington must do – call Hamilton back in "Guns and Ships." By this song he's reached a level of expertise, clear from his language. His actor, Daveed Diggs, notes that "Lafayette has to figure it out. Lafayette is rapping in a real like simple early eighties style rap cadence at first and then by the end he's doing his crazy double and triple time things" (*Hamilton's America*). As Miranda puts it, "He goes from being one of Hamilton's friends to a rap god/military superhero" once he's put in command (*Hamilton: The Revolution* 119).

Historically, Hamilton considered Lafayette invaluable. "The United States are under infinite obligations to him beyond what is known," he said, "not only for his valor and good conduct as major general of our army but for his good offices and influence in our behalf with the court of France" (*Papers of Alexander Hamilton*, vol. 1, 563). Without him, there would have been no French troops. "Lafayette agreed to serve without pay, brought a ship to America outfitted at his own expense, and spent lavishly from his own purse to clothe and arm the patriots" (Chernow 96).

Eliza helps Hamilton with his coat when he departs on this new adventure, and Washington gives him a sword, paralleling the previous scene with the pen but promoting him at last. Washington then gives him touching paternal advice:

> Let me tell you what I wish I'd known
> When I was young and dreamed of glory:
> You have no control:
> Who lives, who dies, who tells your story

As he warns Hamilton, something else that will resonate through the musical, "History has its eyes on you." Of course, he is the most written-about Founding Father and here, he invites Hamilton into that story, while warning him of its responsibilities. Hamilton leaps to accept. Considering the moment's significance, Chernow explains:

And Hamilton finally had this moment that he had craved since boyhood – he led the first infantry charge at Yorktown under the glare of these exploding shells. Again, it shows how courageous, almost crazy, Hamilton was in terms of this derring-do. That this rather slight and bookish guy is suddenly this daredevil on the battlefield. (*Alexander Hamilton: American Experience*)

Hamilton was the first to breach the British defenses. Biographer Thomas Fleming adds: "He was absolutely fearless. He got down in the ditch and the Germans, who were defending the redoubt, were firing right into their faces, and he climbed up on the shoulders of his men and got up on the parapet and was dueling with them sword to sword" (*Alexander Hamilton: American Experience*).

The ensemble member who plays the Bullet at the musical's end offers foreshadowing from the beginning. Ariana DeBose, the original Bullet (identifiable by a poof of curls atop her head), said, "I always know I'm aiming for him—even if the rest of the ensemble members don't. So even if I'm just a lady in a ball gown at a party, there's still a part of my character that knows that *that* moment is going to come" (Corde). In "My Shot," she unfreezes last during the "I imagine death so much it feels more like a memory" monologue. She stands beside Hamilton in "Ten Duel Commandants" at numbers six through seven, and he looks at her, anticipating the show's final duel as he brushes death.

After "You'll Be Back," she steps forward for the first time as a spy receiving a letter, only to have her neck snapped by a redcoat and become the first death of the revolution. However, unlike the rest of the ensemble, who return to the anonymous chorus until their next role, the Bullet never seems to leave that first moment behind. Her next appearance as a singular character is in "Stay Alive," when she becomes the actual Bullet for the first time as she passes Hamilton by at the sound of the gunshot at the top of the song, and from that moment on, every second she is allowed the audience's full or even partial attention, she becomes a harbinger of death. (Corde)

The ghost ensemble crowded around Hamilton mime being shot, emphasizing responsibility. "Who?" demand the circling ensemble lit in brown like the multiracial soldiers while Hamilton and Washington stand in the middle, brightly lit. Soldiers march and line up behind Hamilton then Washington. He orders his troops in their red and blue coats and thus is set apart from them as responsible commander. All this contrasts with the British in bright redcoats. Amid the powerful lyrics "And his right hand man," Washington raises his sword.

Hamilton's rap style works especially well here as he barks orders. His troops semicircle around him singing, "I am not throwing away my shot." Then as he raps more, the troops provide backup with dramatic gestures. Red lights echo shooting.

Eliza stands on the balcony in a sage gown reading his letters as he recalls with a twist on meaning, "My Eliza's expecting me/not only that, my Eliza's expecting." Thus he makes unorthodox plans:

> We gotta go, gotta get the job done
> Gotta start a new nation, gotta meet my son!
> Take the bullets out your gun!

He makes the surprising decision that his men should unload their guns to ensure a stray shot doesn't give them away. This is historically accurate, though Miranda notes this also marks Hamilton as a "control freak" (*Hamilton: The Revolution* 121). Aside from being clever, this is a soft note of pacifism on the edge of war.

Over all, Hamilton did gestures just as mad-looking as this one. Before the battle, Hamilton engaged in a reckless show of bravado. Freeman explains:

> He's so desperate to prove himself that he goes a little over the edge, and he deliberately drills his men in full sight of the enemy. To the point that the enemy says, well this must be a trick, right? Because no one would actually be so stupid as to drill his men in front of us without there being a

trap of some kind. (*Alexander Hamilton: American Experience*)

Thus, though they were in range, the perplexed British soldiers didn't fire. The soldiers advance…their password Rochambeau was chosen because it sounded like "Rush on, boys!"

Hercules Mulligan in his ski cap reveals himself dramatically in the mist of the battle of Yorktown – he bursts from the center of the dancers as they all wave red British coats. In fact, Hercules has been hidden in plain sight. He reveals he's been

> A tailor spyin' on the British government!
> I take their measurements, information and then I smuggle it…To my brother's revolutionary covenant
> I'm runnin' with the Sons of Liberty and I am lovin' it!

The Battle of Yorktown begins. The fighting is dramatic with red-trimmed navy coats for the patriots. Breakdancing and twirling rifles add the manly showing off that's long been linked with both battle and performance. Red light and swirling guns punctuate the battle as well as cries of "what" that sound like "shot" with all its meanings. The cast end dramatically frozen with guns pointing.

The battle finishes in silence. Hamilton narrates the surrender – a single white flag spied after a week. Then with growing volume the ensemble sing about "a world turned upside down" as the heroes individually burst out "we won." Each plants himself on a table or chair with Hamilton on his soapbox – it echoes the tavern celebrations but much stiller. It's a stunned moment, and an uncertain one. The light turns golden brown like dawn, but it's striped with shadows like gravestones or bars – there's still darkness. The Schuyler sisters appear on the edges, emphasizing this is their war too.

"A world turned upside down" has multiple meanings – they are in a revolution and the chaos of war, but also they are trying to flip the world and govern themselves. This phrase is actually a lyric from a British drinking song of the time, reimagined for the show (Miranda and McCarter, *Hamilton: The Revolution* 123). Mary J. Blige's version of "I'm Going Down," with the lyric, "My whole world's turned upside down" also echoes some of the tones.

The number feels like the final number of Act One – the war, which has been the goal since the third song, has been won. But if this is the story of Hamilton's ambition and the creation of the new country, there's a bit more to do.

The success at Yorktown ends in a moment of triumph – true, the world has been turned upside down, but the heroes have succeeded. By contrast, most musicals offer a more foreboding exit note. "This is how an act traditionally ends: in a crisis that seems completely beyond redemption. It's why we come back for Act Two" (Viertel 158). The Phantom of the Opera brings down the chandelier or the neighborhood of *Rent* is being demolished. Thus more story follows.

Aftermath

After Yorktown, the last songs emphasize the mistakes the fledgling country is primed to make – this is not just a story of war but one of Hamilton's rise to politics and all the trials along the way. In fact, there still is no united country, with the Constitution yet to be written. America had to prove it could function without a king or an aristocracy – concepts unseen in the world to date.

Hamilton takes a moment to meet his son, and he and Burr vulnerably greet their children side by side in waistcoats and white shirtsleeves. When Hamilton discovers in the same scene that Laurens has died, he rushes away from the domestic scene, insisting, "I have so much work to do." Act II with its journey to forming the country is beginning.

Laurens perished attacking the British in August 1782 at only age 27, as one of the last casualties of the war. Washington named him "intrepidity bordering on rashness" (Wallace 489). His death was a true devastation for Hamilton, who never found another comrade as close. "Despite a large circle of admirers, Hamilton did not form deep friendships easily and never again revealed his interior life to another man as he had with Laurens" (Chernow 173).

In "Non-Stop," Burr and Hamilton become lawyers, donning navy and green coats to show new roles once again. They dress themselves – taking their own power at last. Burr's coat is noticeably darker as once again the men dress as opposites. They stand in light squares, but these are not side-by-side as they were in the previous scene – the lights are different colors and set at angles to each other – not just offices but jarringly different ones, suggesting different styles of law.

> Thus, from the outset of their careers, Hamilton and Burr were thrust into close proximity and a competitive situation. Both were short and handsome, witty and debonair, and fatally attractive to women. Both young colonels had the self-possession of military men, liked to flaunt their titles, and seemed cut out to assume distinguished places at the New York bar. Yet in the public sphere, Burr already trailed his upstart acquaintance, who was now a hero of Yorktown and basked in the reflected aura of General Washington. (Chernow 169)

The lights transform to a circle of Hamilton's courtroom, though once more there's the suggestion of a target, blending motifs from war to court. Burr introduces the lyrics and music of Hamilton's writing "like you're running out of time" in a bouncy, Caribbean-beat samba-reggae number. The staging is a whirlwind of spinning as Hamilton rushes from activity to activity, lecturing fellow politicians in their chairs, writing at his desk, defending a client in court. A green light for Hamilton writing and doing legal business appears as a new motif. As it happens, the real Hamilton's study was also money green. He wrote constantly, carrying a portable writing desk everywhere, even on horseback (*Hamilton's America*).

Hamilton had a vision of a united America, not just thirteen loosely allied states. From the Caribbean as he was, he had more loyalty to the abstract concept of America than to one city. Freeman adds, "Hamilton is really, remarkably, one of the first – and certainly the most persistent person – calling for a stronger government, a more organized, centralized, national government of some kind. He's really sort of out there in a way that's just really noticeable" (*Alexander Hamilton: American Experience*).

In "Nonstop" he stands determinedly on a table and lectures the other Founding Fathers. He and Burr work as a team (though often disagreeing) until Hamilton asks Burr to write the Federalist Papers defending the Constitution. There's no proof Hamilton asked Burr to write the Federalist Papers but Miranda found the idea intriguing. "This is the equivalent of asking someone to invest in Pixar just before *Toy Story* drops" (*Hamilton: The Revolution* 138). Of course, cautious Burr rejects the risky endeavor. Historian Gordon S. Wood adds:

> The Anti-Federalists, or those opposed to the Constitution, are frightened of the very things that the Patriots in the 1760s had been frightened of. They had just thrown off Great Britain, 3,000 miles away, and now they're re-imposing on themselves this powerful government with a kind of an elected king – and we can see the presidency is a, you know, enormously powerful office. They were frightened of all that, because this was a violation of everything the Revolution had been about. (*Alexander Hamilton: American Experience*)

Together with James Madison and John Jay, Hamilton won the crowd over with his articles, *The Federalist Papers*, which appeared in newspapers over seven months. Carol Berkin notes: "He really is a master in this convention of winning people over, beating people down, wearing people out, stalling. And finally, issuing a few well-placed threats that turn the convention, which should have voted no, into a yes convention" (*Alexander Hamilton: American Experience*).

In New York City, April 30, 1789, George Washington took the oath of office as the country's first president under the new constitution.

The final song brings back many motifs from the show, from all of Eliza and Angelica's perspectives (complete with their melodies) to Burr's jealousy and determination to "wait for it." There's rivalry couched in "Aaron Burr, Sir," and Hamilton finally claims his shot. The music interrupts the Caribbean beat to interject everything from melodic piano to record scratching as the story arcs converge.

This intersection of plotlines and characters with their theme songs echoes "One Day More" from *Les Mis*, especially, as everyone continues their agenda while hoping the new world post-revolution will be better than the old one. Of course, as with this song, or with "La Vie Boheme" from *Rent*, there's a touch of melancholy and loss. The same mood appears in the chaotic Act I ending of Miranda's *In the Heights*. As Viertel adds, "We're left with the sense that the entire structure of the community we've come to know and care about is on a precipice and not about to stop moving forward. Whether it will go completely over a cliff remains to be seen" (171).

Continuing the theme of parting, Angelica sails away (literally on the blue-pattern turntable) to be married. Her leaving means the departure of his last companion – Lafayette and Mulligan do not appear again. With Laurens gone, it's as if Hamilton's idealism has died as well. On cue, Eliza floats up to counsel him to be happy with what he has. The two sisters always appear thus, each tugging at one side of him. Angelica has made an ambitious marriage and still admires Hamilton's intellect while Eliza hopes he will settle down.

Literally a minute later, Washington offers him the position of Secretary of the Treasury, looking down from the catwalk on one side, while Eliza begs him to come home from the other side. Act I ends with a Schuyler sister persuading him on either side and Washington above, so Hamilton looks visually torn.

Hamilton called his ambition a "love of fame, the ruling passion of the noblest minds, which would prompt a man to plan and undertake extensive and arduous enterprises for the public benefit" (*Papers of Alexander Hamilton*, vol. 4, 615). Indeed, his craving to prove himself, urge to leave a legacy and interest in creating a great country all converge here, and Eliza's hopes crumple.

He climbs the stairs, ascending to accept Washington's job and adventure with a defiant protest of "I am not throwing away my shot!" Historically, he was age 34.

Hamilton and Washington almost perfectly mesh and complement each other. Washington was intelligent but not an intellectual, he was not an original policy thinker. With Washington and Hamilton, we have the union of the greatest politician of the day with the greatest policymaker of the day. (*Alexander Hamilton: American Experience*)

Chernow explains: "Washington is allowing, indeed encouraging, Hamilton to function as something more like a prime minister. So that when you say to people that Hamilton was the first treasury secretary, it doesn't quite capture the magnitude of his power – or why Hamilton was so controversial" (*Alexander Hamilton: American Experience*). Quite soon he was to institute a national currency, establish the forerunner of the Federal Reserve, and encourage the growth of the stock market. He also reached beyond the financial post to advocate for a national army and coast guard.

With this new chapter in his life arriving, Act I ends.

ACT II

Enter Jefferson

With a purple coat and exaggerated swagger, Jefferson enters by descending a staircase with far more pomp than Hamilton once did: Washington has appointed the former minister to France as secretary of state. His slaves line up adoringly, prepared to back up his song.

"Thomas Jefferson is a little older, so he dresses like Morris Day and sings jazzy R&B" (Hiatt). He echoes Prince, or any other celebrity fop. Miranda explains:

> It's about eliminating distance. If your mission is to make a story that happened 200-odd years ago resonate with contemporary audiences, what are the ways in which you can eliminate distance? And, man, does that purple suit with a frilly blouse do that. Just like when we pull out those microphones for that Cabinet battle. It's the only anachronistic prop in the show. (Binelli)

Historically, Jefferson actually overdressed and designed his own special soldiers' uniforms.

"What'd I miss?" he asks arrogantly, dancing amid his servants as the light turns red. (In a sly joke, "What'd I miss" echoes the theatergoers back late from intermission.) With the crowd of attendants and the red and purple light and clothing, he parallels King George and his privilege. The chorus drag his staircase around in a way that disturbingly echoes slavery's manual labor, and Jefferson addresses his slave mistress Sally Jenkins – the ugliness of the Founding Fathers is fully on display. The historical Hamilton writes of

67

Jefferson's arrogance and hatred of a central government:

> In France he saw government only on the side of its
> abuses....He came here probably with a too partial idea of
> his own powers and with the expectation of a greater share
> in the direction of our councils than he has in reality
> enjoyed. I am not sure that he had not peculiarly marked
> out for himself the department of the finances. He came
> electrified plus with attachment to France, and with the
> project of knitting together the two countries in the closest
> political bands.... ("Letter to Edward Carrington")

James Madison greets him, eager for help. Madison was a very wealthy plantation owner who dressed like a parson. He served in Congress during the war instead of the front lines. He'd never done manual labor.

In fact, Madison had been Hamilton's ally in the fight to ratify the new Constitution, but he and Thomas Jefferson came to prefer power for state governments. As early as 1792, Hamilton complained, "Mr. Madison cooperating with Mr. Jefferson is at the head of a faction decidedly hostile to me and my administration" ("Letter to Edward Carrington"). Miranda notes that this split occurs during the intermission.

To pass the Constitution, Madison spoke at Virginia's Ratifying Convention, countering Patrick Henry's emotional rhetoric with logic and facts he and Hamilton had worked out. He also vowed to balance the Constitution with the Bill of Rights, which he drafted (a point Madison quickly interjects in "Washington on Your Side"). Madison was soon elected to Congress. However, once there, Madison led Congress's unsuccessful attempt to block Hamilton's national bank and other Federalist projects. He went on to be the fourth President of the United States from 1809 to 1817. Ironically, during the War of 1812, he had difficulty because of the weak national army and bank, so after, he came closer to Hamilton's point of view.

With Madison fully clothed in grey and Jefferson in plum, the characters have graduated from the ensemble's white suits to be fully actualized. They won't keep switching roles but will stay politicians for all of Act II. The coat changes suggest growth as well as the passage of time – new outfits mean new roles and responsibilities. Washington wears stately black with Hamilton now fully in green. Hamilton adds glasses eventually, showing his age by the end. Green nods to his treasury role and financial success. The green also sets him in opposition to Jefferson, whose loose hair, long purple coat, and velvet waistcoat all stress his love of luxury.

Of course, Hamilton hasn't learned to be smooth and gracious. Chernow comments, "He's so capable, so kind of self-consciously brilliant in a way, that he makes an amazing number of enemies" (*Alexander Hamilton: American Experience*). Berkin adds:

> He was really sort of the bull in the china shop. I think one of his greatest difficulties was that, time and time again, he proved he was smarter than other people, and so he could not understand why they didn't shut up and listen to him. He had very little training in the art of politics as a young man. I mean, think about all of these men of the revolutionary generation. Their fathers were in the colonial legislature, their grandfathers were. Politics was talked about at the dinner table. You heard mistakes that people made. You learned finesse. Hamilton never had that. (*Alexander Hamilton: American Experience*)

Moments after their introduction, Hamilton starts a rap battle with Jefferson...with Washington as the referee. "The rap battles, I think, are 'you think our country should be like this, our country should be like that,' and if you win, our country goes to ruins" Miranda adds ("Hamilton: A Founding Father"). Hip-hop is important for a war of ideas since "we get more language per measure than any other musical form" ("Hip-hop and History Blend"). Thus the battles are some of the most popular scenes, perfectly reimagined for the contemporary era. Washington addresses the audience directly, inviting them to participate and welcoming them to the show.

Explaining the predicament they were debating, Berkin notes:

> We owed money to our own army. We owed money to the officers of the army, many of whom had spent their entire fortunes equipping and taking care of the regiments that they had put together. We owed little old ladies who had given over supplies and horses to the army and gotten a piece of paper that said, "we'll pay you for this." We couldn't pay them. So there was no confidence in the government, there was no confidence in the economy. And so we were in a serious economic depression, and no one was certain how to get out of it. (*Alexander Hamilton: American Experience*)

Chernow adds:

> It would have been easy enough, and almost predictable, for a revolutionary government to repudiate that debt. But Hamilton felt that unless the debt was paid off, the United States would never be able to borrow money again, and that this would weaken it as a great power. Hamilton had developed this theory that unless you could establish the credit of the state, you could never have a mighty country…He felt that if the federal government assumed the debt from the states, that all of the creditors would feel that they had a direct financial stake in the survival of the still shaky, new federal government – because that became the government that was going to pay them off. (*Alexander Hamilton: American Experience*)

Thus Hamilton fights for national responsibility for the states' debts. Jefferson believed that America's success lay in its classic farming tradition. Hamilton favored more innovative manufacture and commerce. In this and basically every other political decision, Hamilton and Jefferson warred, to a personal degree. Hamilton writes:

> In the question concerning the Bank, he not only delivered an opinion in writing against its constitutionality and expediency, but he did it in a style and manner which I felt as partaking of asperity and ill humor towards me. As one of the trustees of the Sinking Fund, I have experienced, in

almost every leading question, opposition from him. When any turn of things in the community has threatened either odium or embarrassment to me, he has not been able to suppress the satisfaction, which it gave him... ("Letter to Edward Carrington")

This animosity appears in the personal insults and anger of the first cabinet rap battle. The brief interlude "No John Trumbull" (cut from the final version of the show) contrasts the famous stately historical painting with the angry, squabbling reality (Dreamcatcher). Indeed, in Trumbull's classic painting *Declaration of Independence*, everyone looks mature, stately and dignified – a far contrast with the anger of the cabinet meeting. Freeman comments:

It's really important to understand the politics of this period, to remember the fact that you don't have institutionalized national political parties at this time, and without parties, without team rules of fighting, politics ends up being very personal, based on character and reputation, and premised largely on the rules of honor, the code of honor. It's very, very personal and thus very volatile. The personal and the political are mixed in with each other in a really interesting and ultimately dangerous kind of a way. ("The Duel")

On the floor, Jefferson smugly quotes his Declaration of Independence, reminding everyone who wrote it. Meanwhile, Hamilton dances around, ridiculing Jefferson. The line "Turn around, bend over/I'll show you where my shoe fits," even provokes Jefferson to rush him as they audience hoot. Meanwhile, an allusion to shooting Hamilton with information provides creepy foreshadowing.

Partisanship

The country continued splitting into factions even as Washington frantically held it together. During Washington's first administration, the Democratic-Republican Party (originally called "Democrats," "Republicans," or "Jeffersonians") advocated for less central government.

71

Hamilton insisted the Constitution offered "implied powers," but the new Democratic-Republicans would have none of it. The Federalist Party emerged in opposition, founded by Hamilton and formed from the bankers and businessmen who admired his ideas such as protective tariffs and a central bank. The Federalists went on to advocate for a 1794 treaty with Britain, a highly controversial decision. By the 1796 election, clear political parties had formed.

Other Federalists included Hamilton's fellow writer of the Federalist Papers John Jay (America's first Chief Justice) and Vice President John Adams. (In Washington's government, John Adams discovered, disconcertingly, that the Vice President had very little to do….hence Hamilton's snark that he doesn't have a "real job.") Washington disliked this fragmentation and insisted he had no party affiliation, but he favored a strong central government as well. Technically Adams went on to be the only Federalist president, as the party dissolved by about 1816.

In 1790, Jefferson was eager to move the seat of government far from the foul air of New York City to an empty stretch on the banks of the Potomac, not far from his plantation in Virginia. Hamilton preferred a New York capitol but was flexible. Further, he was willing to sacrifice much to pass his treasury plan.

Historian Richard J. Payne clarifies: "I think this goes back again to Hamilton the outsider. He isn't from New York, he's a West Indian. And so he's willing to sacrifice state and local interests for the broader national purpose, a strong United States. If that meant sacrificing New York, he'd do it – and he did it" (*Alexander Hamilton: American Experience*). At last, Jefferson and Hamilton agreed to meet for dinner at Jefferson's house on Maiden Lane to talk out their differences with James Madison in attendance. The result was one of the most famous meals in American history – the Dinner Table Compromise.

Hamilton and Burr begin "The Room Where it Happens" by joking about death and General Mercer's monument – all quips that foreshadow the end. To Burr's surprise, Hamilton intends to get his debt plan passed through a simple method: "I guess I'm gonna fin'ly have to listen to you...Talk less. Smile more," he sings, parodying Burr. Burr is annoyed however when Hamilton's strategy works – he is now wielding Burr's superpowers as well as his own. Worse yet, Burr is excluded from the fateful decision-making.

Miranda's mantra for the show was "the political always has to be personal" ("Hip-hop and History Blend"). Upon finding Burr has taken her father's senate seat, there's a cut scene where Eliza goes to find Hamilton, noting, "He'll consider this a personal slander – I gotta stop a homicide!" (Dreamcatcher). This emphasizes the depth of his anger and foreshadows that Burr and Hamilton's rivalry will lead to murder. There's also emphasis on Hamilton's pride and sense of personal injury. Eliza sings "Let it Go" directly after, to counter Hamilton who's planning to publish scathing letters against Burr – more foreshadowing for the ending. "People will always be critical. They'll always try to make the personal political," she says, setting up the Reynolds scandal. Her line "You don't have to bring a gun to a knife fight" also foreshadows the end. At the same time, the song is very repetitive, and only reemphasizes the Burr-Hamilton rivalry.

Onstage, Miranda emphasizes Burr's misery at not being involved. Madison, Hamilton, and Jefferson shut themselves in a light square, excluding Burr out in the dark. The ensemble dance in more squares around him, once more shutting him out. "What do you want?" the ensemble cry, referencing the trading going on around a now-circular red table, with Burr stuck creeping around the edge of its spotlight. "I want to be in the room where it happens," Burr responds, swept away by the meeting he isn't part of. Miranda explains that the song is "the turning point for Burr to stop hanging back on his heels and lean forward and say 'I want in on this life'" (*Hamilton's America*).

Inside, in their purple, green, and grey, the trio reach accord, all silently, dramatically clinking fine glasses. By contrast, "The Room Where it Happens" has the exiled Burr dancing all alone, with the ensemble as his backup but not a part of his story. Purple lights and sexy dancing from the ensemble highlight Burr, who in his black coat looks rather devilish. It's a showstopper as he demands to be included. He finally gets into the room, where he dances, even jumping on the table, but only after their meeting is finished. Thus he begins to plot.

Meanwhile, Hamilton's immigrant status, a source of celebration in Act I as Hamilton fights for the land of opportunity, becomes an insult. Jefferson and Madison sneer that "this immigrant isn't somebody we chose." Burr contrasts Hamilton with these smug politicians, quipping, "What happens when two Virginians and an immigrant walk into a room?" Burr argues in the Reynolds Affair that Hamilton will be condemned even more for being an "immigrant embezzling our government funds." Thus as John Adams labels him a "Creole bastard" and Burr calls him an "immigrant bastard," his origins become nasty insults.

When Britain and France went to war in 1793, the U.S. was caught in the middle. The 1778 treaty of alliance with France was still in effect, yet the United States traded heavily with Britain. Hamilton favored the country with commerce, while Jefferson was devoted to France where he'd spent so much of his life.

A further complication was the French Revolution in 1789. As they modeled themselves after the American one, especially with its Declaration of the Rights of Man (which Jefferson advised Lafayette on) many Americans sympathized. Of course, their revolution became known for its violent excesses as the angry commoners guillotined all aristocrats and their sympathizers. Paris was consumed by riots, chaos, and widespread looting as revolution followed revolution.

In the show's second rap battle (this one about sending military aid to Revolutionary France and the Neutrality Act of 1793) all the Founding Fathers make valid points – the

French Revolution is worthy, as Jefferson insists. However, Hamilton points out that America's treaty with the dead King of France is now invalid. Washington hesitates to involve his young country in every foreign war.

A third cabinet battle tackled slavery but didn't actually reveal much about the characters and got cut. "This is the stain on our soul and democracy," Hamilton insists (*Hamilton: The Revolution*, 213). On the other hand, Jefferson's point "We cannot cure prejudice or righteous, desperate hate," is true as well (212). Washington was uncertain (though a slave owner, he did free his slaves upon his death) but concluded it was too volatile an issue to address, a viewpoint that laid the ground for the later Civil War.

After their face off, Jefferson sings and raps, annoyed, about having "Washington on your side." The song begins lit in red, then as the men plan, the lights flash and cries of "oh" resemble cannon fire. The ensemble line up behind Jefferson, Madison, and Burr like an army – political warfare is reaching a new level here.

Historian Karl F. Walling comments: "Washington gave Hamilton credibility. People will do what Hamilton wants because Washington says you can trust him. If there's no Washington, they will not trust Hamilton" (*Alexander Hamilton: American Experience*). Thus Washington's retirement leaves Hamilton in a precarious position. Washington and Hamilton say their goodbyes both in black with shirtsleeves – vulnerable and casual as well as identical – working as a team as they did in the war.

Washington equates the Bible with peace and references Micah 4:4: "Everyone will sit under their own vine and under their own fig tree, and no one will make them afraid," as his image of the perfect retirement in the new world he's helped build. To him, God is a protector, not an instrument of vengeance. Washington then sings the lights out, suggesting his quiet death.

The cut song "One Last Ride" shows the Whiskey Rebellion and has Washington and Hamilton heroically

75

leading the army into battle to end it (as happened historically) amid a reprise of "Here comes the president" and "You are outgunned, outmanned, outnumbered, outplanned!" Washington's stately presence instantly quells the fighting while Hamilton mouths off behind him. It's an interesting event (though literally a minute long), but doesn't necessarily help the main story. Already, Washington is a force of intimidation and command, already Hamilton is a war hero struggling to hold the country together.

John Adams, George Washington, and Thomas Jefferson quitting their jobs didn't happen at exactly the same time – there was a three year gap. Hamilton didn't precisely retire, either – while returning to his legal practice, he organized charities in New York and became a leader of an abolition movement – through his actions, slavery was phased out and forbidden in New York.

In *Hamilton: The Revolution*, Miranda cites the HBO miniseries on John Adams, which inspired the king's comment about meeting Adams when he was an ambassador to Britain. In the scene, Adams is mousy and terrified. George barely says a word, but finally utters icily, "I pray, Mr. Adams, that the United States does not suffer unduly from its want of monarchy." In "I Know Him," the king consequently sings:

> That's that little guy who spoke to me
> All those years ago
> What was it, eighty-five?
> That poor man, they're gonna eat him alive!

In 1798, President John Adams appointed the aging Washington general of the American forces as hostilities rose between America and France. (This was called the Quasi-War.) Washington turned down Burr's application to be a brigadier general and wrote, "By all that I have known and heard, Colonel Burr is a brave and able officer, but the question is whether he has not equal talents at intrigue"

(Lomask 215). He appointed Hamilton as his second-in-command instead, despite Adams' animosity towards him. Hamilton served as Inspector General of the Army, and took over command upon the death of Washington in 1799.

Adams and Hamilton had quite the historical animosity, as Hamilton had favored a different Federalist candidate. During the presidency, Hamilton did not deal directly with Adams, but he continued to advise cabinet members. By 1800, Adams feared they were taking orders from Hamilton rather than himself. He disbanded the army Hamilton had fought to create and removed the two members of his cabinet who had defended Hamilton's policies.

Hamilton responded angrily. His *Letter ... Concerning the Public Conduct and Character of John Adams*, published before the election of 1800, helped block Adams' reelection. It began, "Not denying to Mr. Adams' patriotism and integrity and even talents of a certain kind," and went on to assert that he was "unfit for the office of Chief Magistrate" on account of lack of sound judgment, eccentricity, inability to persevere, vanity beyond bounds, and "a jealousy capable of discoloring every subject" (Johnson 241). Hamilton may have planned to circulate the document only among his own party, but Aaron Burr ensured that it spread, dooming Adams and ruining Hamilton's own career (Johnson 242).

The John Adams presidency doesn't get much emphasis in the show – Miranda actually cut Hamilton's song about it and only left the last line, "Sit down, John, you fat mother –" Though the end is bleeped out, red lights flash like a siren, and it's clear Hamilton (standing up on the balcony and pronouncing fate) has bombed his own political career with the attack. In a released clip, Hamilton raps about the "arrogant, anti-charismatic embarrassment known as John Adams" in the rap version of his published letter. He also insults Abigail – something the audience didn't care for and one reason the song was pulled. Mostly, however, it was a long time to spend on a character never seen onstage.

So much for Adams. Spurred by his new ambition, Burr

joins Jefferson and Madison in complaining about Hamilton and they add a crowd dancing behind them in support…then the trio plot to bring him down with the Reynolds Affair.

Wife, Sister, Maria

As Hamilton hurls himself into politics, his writing desk and Phillip's piano twirl on the turntable in parallel to each other. He's reluctant to take a moment to see their son perform. At the same time, he enjoys corresponding with Angelica, and in fact neglects his wife and child while writing to her. (His references to *Macbeth* will also prove prophetic.) As they correspond, wife-Eliza is lit in the blue of sorrow, her Act II color, while Angelica is cheerful in a peachy-pink light. Both women flirt, with lots of touching and closeness. While sometimes they offer the same message to Hamilton (stressing how important it is, as it's repeated) most often they contrast, with one happy while the other is sad or one tongue-tied, one talkative. They're his anima, but also a yin-yang pair, reflecting opposite sides of the self. Their music also contrasts as each repeats her own themes. Lacamoire explained:

> I use the cello for two characters: Burr and Angelica. That shows how versatile it is. The cello can be really snaky and sinister when you want it to, like on "Say No to This." On "Wait for It," the cello gives this little hint of the melody. It matches Leslie's voice, which is really silky. Angelica also has a lot of cello moments, and the harp. When we get to the finale, Eliza starts talking about Angelica, I'm like, *all right, we need to do something to echo her themes,* so you hear that line from "Satisfied" again on the harp. It's about finding a way to evoke her when her name is called. The violin represents Eliza. In "That Would Be Enough," there's a high violin that echoes her part. Same thing in the finale: When she talks about the orphanage, there's a tender violin line. Hamilton is so kinetic and percussive and propulsive, and Eliza's very organic and not electric. A lot of her moments don't have any synth instruments. "That

Would Be Enough" is totally chamber, acoustic instruments. Same thing with "Burn," it's very chamber-y. (Jones)

Angelica visits and the women unite to tell him "take a break" but even confronted by the pair – love and ambitious passion tugging on each arm as they did before – he refuses them both. From "Nonstop" and through this scene, Hamilton and Eliza both wear green, emphasizing their united couple status even as he takes her for granted and pursues the more colorful Angelica. He then falls into the clutches of the bad girl, Maria, dressed all in sexy crimson against the murky swirling light.

In the summer of 1791, when Alexander Hamilton was thirty-six years old, his family, now with five children, had moved to Philadelphia. With them all on vacation in Albany, a lovely woman in distress arrived at his door. Author Willard Sterne Randall adds:

> She said she was from New York and she knew Hamilton was, and she needed a way to get home to her family. Her husband had abandoned her, she didn't have any money, was there anything that he could do to help her. So he went around that night with a bank draft to her boardinghouse. The draft would be worth about four hundred dollars today. Went up the back stairs, not the front. Knocked on her door. She ushered him into her bedroom and pretty quickly made it plain that there were other ways that she could repay him for his generosity. And he kept going back for thirteen months, and she kept repaying him for thirteen months. (*Alexander Hamilton: American Experience*)

The lighting is mostly dark purple on a duplicitous black stage. Hamilton's literal prayer, for the strength to resist temptation, fails, as he soon gives into Maria: "Lord, show me how to say no to this/I don't know how to say no to this/Cuz the situation's helpless/And her body's screaming, 'Hell, yes'" ("Say No to This"). The antithesis of "Lord" and "Hell" side by side suggest he's teetering on the brink…and soon succumbs. God is also invoked in a scene of sin, not selflessness, adding to the inappropriateness of only turning to God so Hamilton can resist sex. It's no wonder his appeal fails.

Hamilton raps and Maria sings her part in R&B – this gives them classic gender roles but also parallels his courtship of Eliza, giving it something of an unwholesome reprise. Lacamoire adds, "On Lin's original demo, that song sounded so greasy: It had that cool trap, double-time hi-hat, it had that sinister-ass bass line, it was on a synth, Lin found those *bicka-ba-bicka-ba-bip* sounds. That one came out of the box just killing" (Jones). *Vibe* described the song as "a '90s slow jam, Usher-style" ("Going H.A.M.").

The ghostly figures of the chorus dance behind and around him, protesting his decision and emphasizing his split longings, but he succumbs. The lights suggest a whirlpool sucking Hamilton down. When Maria's husband (in something that might be a red cowboy hat or modern "pimp hat") blackmails him, Hamilton and Maria sing the word "helpless," contrasting them to Eliza. If Eliza in green is his perfect match, Maria's bright red makes her visually clash.

Onstage, she pleads that she had no idea her husband had such a scheme in mind. Chernow notes that the history is far different than her claims: "There seems little question that she approached Hamilton as part of an extortion racket, delivering an adept performance as a despairing woman. It was also clear, however, that she was too flighty to stick to any script (366-367). As she pathetically whined in her letters (characterized by bad spelling and grammar), "Oh my God I feel more for you than myself and wish I had never been born to give you so much unhappisness do not rite to him [her husband] no not a Line but come here soon do not send or leave any thing in his power Maria" (*Papers of Alexander Hamilton,* vol. 10 p378-379). Thus she, like Eliza, truly is helpless, but rather than the good wife, she's a predator who destroys him.

Of course, Hamilton's rivals confront him – historically, they were other characters, but Jefferson, Madison, and Burr make sense here. To prove his innocence, Hamilton pulls out his love letters from Maria and shamelessly insists that his visitors read them. Freeman adds:

> He says, oh no no no, those little slips of paper in which I'm paying money – those I'm not doing anything with government funds, I'm actually paying blackmail because I'm sleeping with his wife. And then he presents them with all sorts of evidence to show them that honestly, it's all about adultery – it's not about public funds at all. And apparently the three gentlemen are, on the one hand, very embarrassed. And on the other hand, they agree – okay, you know, we're sorry, we misunderstood, we'll just keep this all between us. (*Alexander Hamilton: American Experience*)

However, the secret got out. At the time, future president James Monroe and Hamilton actually prepared to duel over Monroe leaking the secret, but Burr, his second, ended the duel before it happened. Different alliances and factions were operating, and some of Hamilton's enemies were eager to exploit the news. In the show it's a malicious blow from the new trio united in tearing him down.

Thus endangered, Hamilton sings "Hurricane" about his need to control his reputation. Close to tears, he recalls his mother's death and then how he "wrote my way out" of poverty. The ensemble are frozen around him, crumpled, then struggling against the blue-purple storm, whisking his desk and chair away like a force of wind. The bursts of chords resemble a pounding gale. The turntable spins, leaving him in the hurricane's glowing eye. Elements of his life and memories all are whirling around him, out of control.

"The last thing that we added was the double turntable," explains set designer David Korins.

> I just couldn't get out of my head the swirling, cyclical motion of the storytelling. It starts with Alexander Hamilton living on the island of Nevis and it gets swept over by a swirling hurricane. That idea, the cyclical swirling continues throughout the themes of the show: including in political

81

struggles, in his sex scandal, the cyclical nature of his
relationship with Burr, and on and on. (Eddy)

In fact, while Burr is locked in with squares, Hamilton's
world is constantly turning, like his quick mind and revolving
circumstances – surprising luck and surprising disaster. His
own cleverness and ego cause one then the other.
    Standing in a hurricane but singing of how he "couldn't
seem to die" is a striking contradiction – even thus beset he is
miserably immortal. Though the crowd advise him "Wait for
it," one, embodying the hurricane, lays a piece of paper
before him. Here we see Hamilton's need to control his
circumstances and his future, to a fault. Chernow adds:

> Hamilton didn't have that judgment that matched the great
> intellect and the great ability. And it's like the flaw of a figure
> in a Greek tragedy, who's headed for a great fall and
> doesn't see it coming. And then, as in a Greek tragedy, you
> sort of look back and you feel that this was bound to
> happen, that this is somehow the logical culmination of
> certain flaws in his personality. (*Alexander Hamilton:
> American Experience*)

In "Schuyler Defeated," Burr shoots the insult "Your
pride will be the death of us all./Beware, it goeth before a
fall" at Hamilton. Of course, this is Proverbs 16:18: "Pride
goes before destruction, a haughty spirit before a fall." While
Burr has already discovered that meekness and faith in God
won't aid him, it is true that Hamilton's pride finally kills him
(though Burr's vengeance on him destroys Burr's own
career). Here, it causes his political fall.
    Hamilton evaluates his life and decides publishing is his
best chance – writing has led to his success but now destroys
him. Miranda orchestrated this turn by revealing "the cracks
in the foundation of his mind" – the ultimate trauma
Hamilton once survived has left him guilty and certain he's
undeserving (*Hamilton: The Revolution* 233). As Chernow
explains further:

> I think that he felt that fate had handed him an opportunity to reinvent himself and to start life over. But I don't think that he ever fully left the world of his childhood behind him. He was poor, he was illegitimate, he was ashamed of all of those things. And even though he tried so hard to escape, on some level he was always trapped back in the darkness of that boyhood. (*Alexander Hamilton: American Experience*)

Thus he created the Reynolds Pamphlet, a long essay explaining the affair and clearing his financial reputation and public life but destroying the personal one. It was "a ninety-five-page booklet: thirty-seven pages of personal confessions, supplemented by fifty-eight pages of letters and affidavits" (Chernow 533).

In *Drunk History*, Miranda calls the Reynolds Pamphlet something of a "Dear Penthouse Forum" letter with gloating, unnecessarily vivid details. Historian Karl F. Walling adds: "Many leaders of the Federalist Party are saying – is that how you're going to defend your ... your honor? You can imagine how much this hurt his wife. The point is Hamilton considered his public honor more important than his private honor" (*Alexander Hamilton: American Experience*). On the one hand Hamilton wrote of his accusers, "With such men, nothing is sacred. Even the peace of an unoffending and amiable wife is a welcome repast to their insatiate fury against the husband" (*Papers of Alexander Hamilton*, vol. 21, p. 239). On the other, it was he who published the pamphlet that so humiliated his wife. He writes:

> This confession is not made without a blush...I can never cease to condemn myself for the pang which it may inflict in a bosom eminently entitled to all my gratitude, fidelity and love. But that bosom will approve that even at so great an expense, I should effectively wipe away a more serious stain from a name which it cherishes with no less elevation than tenderness. (*Papers of Alexander Hamilton*, vol. 21, p. 243-244)

Clearing his good name outweighed Eliza's own. Worse,

Jefferson wrote that Hamilton's "willingness to plead guilty to adultery seems rather to have strengthened rather than weakened the suspicions that he was in truth guilty of the speculations" (qtd. in Chernow 535). The pamphlet scandalized the people and they became disgusted with their hero. Fleming adds: "Jefferson and Madison couldn't believe their eyes. It was the most ... one of the most self-destructive things they ever saw anybody do, and they just rubbed their hands. They really, more or less, realized Hamilton was finished" (*Alexander Hamilton: American Experience*). "My God!" Jefferson bursts on the show.

The enemy trio smirk "Well, he's never gon' be President now" – America has its first sex scandal. "His poor wife!" they conclude. The light goes romantic pink through energetic gold (blending romance and action), but the music, condemning. As the pamphlet circulates, lights flash and speakers boom, like thunder and lightning. The explosion of the stage effects suggests Hamilton has blown up his own world. Meanwhile, Jefferson flings pamphlets about and even gives one to the conductor in the orchestra pit. As he dances gleefully, papers fall over the stage like trash.

This music has "a skittish, double-time strip club anthem beat, as if the Richard Rodgers stage was the Atlanta flesh palace Magic City" (Tommasini and Caramanica). Even King George is dancing in the corner, smirking at America's moral tumble.

At last, Angelica arrives, but the ensemble pelts Hamilton with the pamphlet as she berates him. "Congratulations," Angelica's cut song, emphasizes how bad an idea the Reynold Pamphlet was: "Y'know, you're the only enemy you ever seem to lose to!" (Dreamcatcher). She taunts him with having "redefined your legacy!" as she tackles Eliza's argument – Eliza insists they don't need one, but the more politically-minded Angelica shows that Hamilton has permanently tainted his – an accurate observation. In the onstage version, she taunts him with "You could never be satisfied./God, I hope you're satisfied." The word, once used for their flirtation, now slices at him. His lust has destroyed his relationship with Angelica as well as with his wife.

All suddenly quiets, and in the stillness, Eliza sings "Burn." The scene cuts to her sitting sadly on her blue-lit stone bench. In a simple white gown, suggesting innocence and vulnerability with its low neckline and brief blue sash, Eliza kneels as if at an altar praying. There's a single lantern on the white stone gravelike bench beside her.

She realizes that the loving letters of their courtship were a lie. Letters have been their downfall this time. Eliza protests:

> You published the letters she wrote you
> You told the whole world how you brought
> This girl into our bed
> In clearing your name, you have ruined our lives

During her song, Eliza quotes Angelica repeatedly, emphasizing that there have always been three people in their marriage. Angelica, meanwhile, has announced, "You have married an Icarus/He has flown too close to the sun" (an actual quote from one of her letters).

It's a minor ballad, longing with strong chords. Eliza's refrain and the song title "Burn" is an insult in modern vernacular, as well as suggesting love, passion, and hope...now all shattered. However, Eliza turns the word into a quiet defiance and moment of destruction – she literally burns their letters onstage, erasing his words and destroying the private, personal memories of their courtship – a life he has just endangered. Her line about being "in the narrative" is back, this time with some consideration of what future historians will think. She chooses to remove her personal pain and sorrow from the story instead of letting the public share them.

"She didn't really have options. She couldn't just leave him. She had eight children," Philippa Soo explains (*Hamilton's America*). Now Eliza takes her revenge with her own letters. "I'm burning the memories/Burning the letters that might have redeemed you," she decides. (Historically, she doesn't seem to have burned their romantic correspondence now, instead choosing much later to leave them out of the "narrative." However, taking revenge using Hamilton's words and legacy is certainly fitting.) "I hope that you burn," she concludes.

Philip

Young Philip has an adorable introduction as he raps in the style of his father on his ninth birthday while Eliza beat-boxes for him. (In an anachronism, Philip raps he wants a little brother. He actually had several by this point.) Hamilton is touched by his prodigy son. Freeman explains: "He, of course, loved all of his children. But I think he had particularly bright hopes for the oldest son, which was Philip. There's something a little rakish about him when you see the image of him from the time – sort of a chip off the old block" (*Alexander Hamilton: American Experience*). Philip and his mother also count together in French, in a pattern that echoes the counting and melody of each duel – a chilling hint of his final fate.

A cut scene, in which Eliza and Philip meet Burr in town in "Schuyler Defeated," would have compared Philip and Theodosia as accomplished adults of the same age, both excelling in Latin and French (Dreamcatcher). This scene seems to foreshadow a happy suitability and perhaps a romance despite their fathers' feuding, subversively preparing the audience for a happy end before the extra shock of Philip's tragedy.

In a bit of a heartbreaking nod, Philip returns to the story with a similar rap, reusing his father's early words from around the same age: "I'm only nineteen but my mind is older." A line of students like his father's battalion form behind him. Philip's song has happy flutes and a rock tune…all slightly dissonant as Philip approaches tragedy.

In 1801, Philip Hamilton got into a heated and very

public argument with an arrogant Republican politician, George I. Eaker. The latter had given a Fourth of July speech calling Jefferson a hero and Hamilton the schemer trying to bring them down – not a comment on the Reynolds Affair but a public insult of Hamilton nonetheless.

In a strange coincidence, historically Philip actually did interrupt the play *The West Indian,* paralleling his father's origins, to challenge Eaker to a duel (Chernow 651). Of course, his interrupting a play leans on the fourth wall. Onstage, as he seeks Eaker, it's the woman who plays the Bullet who, significantly, tells Philip where to find his opponent.

As emotional and reckless as young Alexander Hamilton was, the musical version of Philip challenges Eaker then goes to see his father who, all in black now, has become an elder statesman like Washington at last. Time keeps turning onwards. Freeman adds:

> Duels – affairs of honor – in this time period are very ritualized and of course, they need to be because they are potentially deadly and because everything is at stake. If your honor is at stake, that's pretty much the entire game. So apparently, Philip went to his father and described what had happened and, and sort of asks his father for advice. Now what happens dad, what do I do? (*Alexander Hamilton: American Experience*)

Hamilton carefully advises his son to delope – fire in the air. Historian Karl F. Walling explains, "And Hamilton says, look, we've envisioned this great political career for you. You know you might be president someday. But you know if you turn down the challenge, you'll be considered a coward and your political career will be over. You'll be a social outcast" (*Alexander Hamilton: American Experience*).

Historically, Philip and his opponent both refused to fire, but after a long, confusing pause, both raised their pistols and Eacker shot. Philip fired (possibly in an involuntary spasm) before slumping to the ground. Onstage, more tragically, Philip is gunned down before the final count. Young men with guns cannot always control their responses.

> The aftermath of the duel had eerie parallels to Hamilton's later confrontation with Burr. Philip's partisans told of his noble but ultimately suicidal resolution not to fire first, and they cursed the rival who had failed to respond in kind. Even the debate over whether Philip had discharged his weapon deliberately or in a spasm of pain was recapitulated later. (Chernow 654)

Further, Philip, who died at 19, lived through 19 songs. Hamilton died at 47, and the musical has roughly 47 songs, depending how one counts.

In this duel, there's no target shape, just white spotlights, but the ensemble in their white suggest the ghosts Philip will join. He's wounded and carried off. His mother arrives, already in black just as Hamilton sings "Stay Alive" to his son, taking the lyrics for himself as he finds himself cast as helpless family, no longer the daredevil hero. The light is the blue of memory and despair as Eliza recalls her son's piano lessons, with the count of ten reimagined from the duel into death. In his own muted grey, Philip shares the touching song with his parents and dies.

In black as well, Angelica, a close outsider like Burr, takes over the narration for a moment. "There are moments that the words don't reach/There is suffering too terrible to name," she sings as the parents stand stunned and silent in black, barely lit in dark purple. The phrases of the song – "working through" and "going through" and "trying to do," paired with "unimaginable," seem vague, but actually emphasize that Hamilton the great writer has no words here. It's something "too terrible to name." The empty streets emphasize how this is a private moment, one so intimate he can't even share his thoughts. Hamilton has envisioned his own death repeatedly, but never this. Freeman adds:

> It's just crushing to Hamilton. His friends talked about how it was stamped on his face, the tragedy of that duel and of Phillip's death, that he never recovered from it. But you can

actually see that in the portraits of him that were painted at that time. (*Alexander Hamilton: American Experience*)

"His hair has gone grey. He passes every day/They say he walks the length of the city," the ensemble sing. The bustling visions of New York have turned empty and isolated, down to the lights and music. Only a pair of strings plays. The ensemble put arms around each other and walk.

In an early draft Burr sang "It's Quiet Uptown, but Miranda explains, "Not only is Angelica the only choice to narrate this moment, it completes her arc in the most unexpected, satisfying way possible. For her to bear witness to the lives of Alexander and Eliza is the role she chose in "Satisfied"...she fulfils it here, at their lowest moment" (*Hamilton: The Revolution*, 203).

Historically, Hamilton found God around this time, and this is reflected in the line "and I pray/that never used to happen before." Ironically, his major prayer scene in "Say No to This," if granted, could have prevented this loss.

Miranda comments, "Hamilton's grange, the house where 'It's Quiet Uptown' takes place, is in the 140s [in New York]. And it was quiet then—this was sort of uncharted land in terms of the city" (Evans). In "It's Quiet Uptown," Hamilton stares at Eliza trying to get through to her, while she resolutely stares ahead. As Hamilton pleads for his wife to stay with him through the pain, he has taken her place as the one who values their domesticity – he sings "That Would Be Enough" and "Look Around" (though this last skips "how lucky we are to be alive right now" in a despondent omission). His line to her, "I'm not afraid – I know who I married," is an act of faith, as hers is in "That Would Be Enough."

When she finally takes his hand, he weeps. They hold each other and cry together, and then they walk the streets together. At last, he puts her first and they move to where "it's quiet uptown." Certainly, Eliza's forgiveness of Hamilton is as important as the loss itself. It takes the sacrifice of their son for Hamilton to welcome love, religion, and all the spirituality both offer back into his life. As this plotline ties up, he withdraws from politics.

With this, the story has nearly ended. Lacamoire explained of "It's Quiet Uptown" "That's the last real ramp-up of story, leading up to the duel. It's the last little mountain-climb" (Jones).

The Final Fight

"Can we get back to politics?" asks Jefferson. Madison agrees, voice rough as if the character has been shaken to the core by the previous few songs (in fact, the actor often has been). He even blows his nose.

To Jefferson's surprise, Madison suggests he get Hamilton's endorsement. The song of "Hamilton's on your side" suggests Hamilton has symbolically stepped into Washington's shoes as older advisor once more. Meanwhile, Burr is canvasing for votes (something that at the time just wasn't done, but he's fully taken Hamilton's advice, it seems). Burr appears thrilled when the people start accepting him as someone they like enough to "share a beer with" – Hamilton is through and he can finally be president without the perpetual thorn in his side. Though the election was contentious, "the happy-go-lucky beat offers a sharp contrast to their verbal sparring" ("Going H.A.M.")

Meanwhile, as the crowd ask Hamilton's opinion, red and white stripes (suggesting not just patriotism but partisanship) spread over the floor. As Burr and Hamilton converse for what seems like the hundredth time (always with "Aaron Burr, sir"), Hamilton has aged and wears glasses and vulnerable-looking white shirtsleeves. "On your side," "talk less/smile more," and "quiet uptown" all reappear.

A "Dear Theodosia" reprise in which Burr's wife dies would have let Burr experience a great loss, paralleling him and Hamilton further (Dreamcatcher). This is another example of how everyone Burr loves dies, adding more pathos to the story. Of course, it also takes focus off Hamilton. Meanwhile, their acquaintance has changed Burr, as Jungian shadow encounters generally do: "I'm chasing what I want…I learned that from you," he reveals.

Jefferson didn't win in a landslide – he tied with Burr. Thus the House had to pick, and Hamilton's endorsement changed the course of the election. Joanne Freeman explains:

> There can't be a worse situation for Hamilton. And, to him, ultimately, there really can be no choice, and he actually says in a wonderful letter, with the longest clause in history written. Okay, Jefferson may be a hypocrite, a fanatic, he doesn't really care about the truth. He has a list of horrible things about Jefferson's character and then goes on to talk about how Jefferson is far superior to Burr. And the reason is because Jefferson cares about what others think about him. He's thinking about his reputation. And so he's not going to act injudiciously. He's not going to dismantle anything. He's going to think before he acts, and he's going to be careful. Burr is not really thinking about fame. He's not thinking, according to Hamilton, about anything other than the moment. And how much power can I get, and how much money can I get. That's how Hamilton sees it. And given that, Burr will do anything he can to get into office, to get those two rewards, including installing himself as an emperor, subverting the constitution. There's no telling what Burr will do once he's in office. So there's no choice between the two men. ("The Duel")

In the musical, Hamilton finally stands on the balcony. Candidates stand below on opposite sides between the crowd, while a red and white ring of light alternate – more partisanship. Either way, all await his opinion and he gives it – "When all is said and all is done/ Jefferson has beliefs. Burr has none." Historian Carol Berkin adds: "Even though he disagreed totally with Jefferson, Jefferson at least was interested in trying to do something that would be good for the United States. Burr – Burr was in it for Burr" (*Alexander Hamilton: American Experience*).

In some ways, Burr was a crook – he offered and took bribes. He collected funds to bring Manhattan clean water then spent them on a bank instead. After Burr took the senate seat from Hamilton's father-in-law (an important backer Hamilton needed to help pass his bills), Hamilton turned savage. "I fear Mr. Burr is unprincipled, both as a public and a private man. In fact, I take it he is for or against nothing but as it suits his interest and ambition," he insisted ("The Duel"). Freeman adds:

> This is the core of what really makes Hamilton so crazed, so really frantically panicked at the idea of Burr in office. It's that Burr is as ambitious as Hamilton is, but there's no restraint. He doesn't appear to be thinking about anything other than what does this opportunity hold? So there's nothing holding him back.

The duel-worthy offense actually came in 1804, after Burr ran for governorship of New York as a member of Hamilton's Federalist Party. "Outraged, Hamilton returned to the political fight. He rode across the state, telling any Federalist who would listen that they should vote for the devil himself before they voted for Burr" ("The Duel"). Burr then ran as an independent but both the Federalists and the Jeffersonians began printing malicious gossip about him. Scholar Thomas Fleming comments:

> He was hammered, to an unbelievable degree, they smeared him in every way you could think of. On the day that the polls opened, the paper published a list of twenty prostitutes, who said that Aaron Burr was their favorite customer. It was the dirtiest political campaign I think probably in the history of the country in terms of personal political attacks. ("The Duel")

Burr lost the election.

Fleming comments, "After Burr lost this unbelievably dirty governorship election, he was a deeply depressed man. We know from his letters to his daughter, that he holed up at his estate, Richmond Hill, and saw nobody, he was isolated" ("The Duel"). Burr needed a path to power and public recognition. The duel was one option. Freeman writes:

> You were not necessarily counting on the fact that you were actually gonna end up with a gun in your hand shooting at someone. You were counting on the fact that you were gonna have a chance to prove that you were willing to die to defend your character! So the code of honor really is being manipulated as a political tool among national politicians in this period, to a really extraordinary degree. ("The Duel")

At a dinner party in March, Hamilton made many rude remarks about his fellow politician. Charles D. Cooper, an attendee at the dinner, published these remarks claiming that Hamilton had called Burr "a dangerous man, and one who ought not be trusted with the reins of government," and that he knew of "a still more despicable opinion which General Hamilton has expressed of Mr. Burr" (Fleming 236). Published and republished, these comments spread. Incensed, Burr demanded Hamilton apologize. He had an excuse for an honorable fight.

In the musical, the light turns red and Burr rages at Hamilton's piece of spite. He sings about his longing for "The Room Where it Happens," this time in his own lit square, but becoming Vice President is a powerless consolation prize and he knows it. Like catty teens, Jefferson and Madison reject his input, and tell him it will be an empty appointment.

Echoing "The Room Where it Happens," the ensemble fix Burr a desk in the light square room where he can begin a letter-feud with Hamilton. "The Bullet actually pulls Burr's desk onto the stage and hands him his quill so that he can begin his fateful letters, edging his toward the battlefield. Every action she takes ensures that Hamilton meets her one last time" (Corde).

"At your service" returns, though this was a popular mode of address. "The serious back and forth banter is set to an almost circus-like instrumental" ("Going H.A.M."). The visuals are also fun as Hamilton pelts a disbelieving Burr with page after page of letters. During their cheeky corresponddence, the signatures are especially singsong-sarcastic, emphasizing the formality of the time with a dash of irony. The men use the same desk and nearly identical signatures, then stand in parallel squares of light, something they haven't done since they greeted their babies. As foils hurtling inevitably toward conflict, their lives still run in parallel, even at the show's end.

In 1804, Hamilton and Burr wrote increasingly antagonistic letters back and forth. As Burr demanded Hamilton assert that he had never said anything derogatory about him (a statement which would have been a lie and also a politically ruinous choice to put in writing), Hamilton quibbled about the ambiguous meaning of "still more despicable," possibly hoping to muddle their quarrel to the point of their both stepping away but in fact further enraging his opponent with his corrections.

BURR:
Sir, I send for your perusal a letter signed by Charles. D. Cooper. You must perceive, Sir, the necessity of a prompt and unqualified acknowledgement or denial of the use of any expressions which could warrant the assertions of Dr. Cooper.
I have the honor to be Your Obedient Servant, Aaron Burr.

HAMILTON:
Sir – The language of Doctor Cooper affirms that I have expressed some opinion "still more despicable," without however mentioning to whom, when, or where. 'Tis evident, that the phrase "still more despicable" admits of infinite shades, from very light to very dark. How am I to judge of the degree intended?
I trust, on more reflection, you will see the matter in the same light with me. If not, I can only regret the circumstance, and must abide the consequences.

BURR:
Sir: The common sense of Mankind affixes to the epithet adopted by Dr. Cooper the idea of dishonor. The question is

WHO TELLS YOUR STORY?

> not whether he has used it with grammatical accuracy, but whether you have uttered expressions derogatory to my honor.
> Your letter has furnished me with new reasons for requiring a definite reply. ("The Duel")

Miranda explains of the letters in the show, "It's Burr looking at his life and saying, 'Wow. At every point along the way, my barrier was you. What do you have to say for yourself?' Hamilton, smart-ass as he is, saying, 'You're gonna have to be more specific than that. I say a lot of shit about you'" (*Hamilton's America*).

He refuses to apologize and proudly agrees to duel. Historian Karl F. Walling comments, "Hamilton, in many ways, is a tragic figure, because the love of honor – which is the source of his greatness, I would argue – is completely consistent with Greek tragedy, also, the source of his downfall" (*Alexander Hamilton: American Experience*). Freeman adds that Hamilton was nearly involved in a duel ten times over his life and always talked his way out of it…until the last (*Hamilton's America*). As Walling concludes, "Hamilton tries to dance with Burr. He comes as close to a full retraction as he could under the circumstances. Burr won't accept it. This indicates to me that Burr really wanted to fight" (*Alexander Hamilton: American Experience*).

On June 27, Burr sent a formal challenge. Onstage, Hamilton bids his wife a brief but touching goodbye before the duel, calling her "the best of wives and the best of women." This song is set to the same melancholy instrumental as "It's Quiet Uptown," emphasizing their sad yet improved relationship. His actual final letter to her is also quite touching:

> [New York, July 4, 1804]
> This letter, my very dear Eliza, will not be delivered to you, unless I shall first have terminated my earthly career; to begin, as I humbly hope from redeeming grace and divine mercy, a happy immortality.

> If it had been possible for me to have avoided the interview, my love for you and my precious children would have been alone a decisive motive. But it was not possible, without sacrifices which would have rendered me unworthy of your esteem. I need not tell you of the pangs I feel, from the idea of quitting you and exposing you to the anguish which I know you would feel. Nor could I dwell on the topic lest it should unman me.
>
> The consolations of Religion, my beloved, can alone support you; and these you have a right to enjoy. Fly to the bosom of your God and be comforted. With my last idea; I shall cherish the sweet hope of meeting you in a better world.
>
> Adieu best of wives and best of Women. Embrace all my darling Children for me.
>
> Ever yours
> A H (*Papers of Alexander Hamilton,* vol. 26, p. 293)

When Hamilton bids Eliza goodbye, she's in a blue dressing gown, suggesting the intimate privacy of their home. Blue is a maternal color, seen in the cloak of the Virgin Mary. Shortly after, she will cast off the robe to return to the white gown. Since her black dress is also an overgown on the white gown, Eliza is the one to now quick-switch roles from happy wife (green) to the betrayed bride of "Burn" (white), to bereft mother (black) to loving but saddened wife (blue) to angelic spirit and eternal biographer (white). It's Hamilton who's stopped changing.

Early morning, July 11, 1804, the duel took place across the Hudson River, in Weehawken, New Jersey. As he boated over, Hamilton gazed back at his growing city and "pointed out the beauties of the scenery and spoke of the future greatness of the city" as one of his sons described it (qtd. in Chernow 701). "Hamilton had calculated (correctly as it turned out) that Burr could not kill him without committing political suicide at the same time" (Chernow 690). Thus he planned to fire in the air or far to Burr's side in emphasis of his nonviolent intentions. He shared this plan with two of his friends (Chernow 690). Burr, meanwhile, practiced at the shooting range and donned a black silk coat that would protect him, at least to a degree, from bullets. Onstage, Hamilton wears a new black coat for the final duel with Burr, as does his nemesis. They are dressed identically as foils with capes that swirl stylishly as the pair circle. Hamilton on stage and history used the same pistols his son had used.

The red and golden target flashes on the floor – action and savagery. "Ten Duel Commandments" returns, blending suspense and inevitability. The audience knows what's coming. Meanwhile, Burr narrates his own thoughts – how Hamilton's soldier prowess makes him a dangerous foe and how much this man has hurt him politically.

Still at this last, Burr cannot understand his rival – "I wish I could tell you what was happ'ning in his brain," insists. Burr is defensive and conflicted. "Hamilton was wearing his glasses/Why? If not to take deadly aim?" a protest he made publically afterwards. He even pleads with the audience for understanding as he protests, "They won't teach you this in your classes."

An earlier version of the duel followed Burr's "Ten Duel Commandments" with counting down from ten to one, beginning a flashback sequence like Angelica's in "Satisfied" (though in fact repeating this feels like a gimmick). Also like Angelica's, this retells the scene from the opposite point of view, allowing Hamilton to share that he planned to delope and only donned glasses to see Burr's face. Repeating this convention didn't particularly improve the story, which was a more interesting twist for Angelica's narrative and this time included Burr's ten steps then Hamilton's ten steps – a long retelling for a second song reprise. The final version allows Hamilton to monologue far more poignantly from the heart, bursting out of the more regimented songs and rhymes in stream of consciousness. It also leaves in history's ambiguities – no one is certain why he wore the glasses or what he was thinking, only what he told others beforehand.

As the turntable goes purple and thorn-covered, the point of view shifts to Hamilton, who has a monologue as time freezes and the bullet slowly fires. The slowness emphasizes time freezing as Hamilton's thoughts race, but also emphasizes inevitability to the viewers. He's on the edge of the wheel with dancers in the middle like images in a wishing well. On creating this final scene, Miranda was inspired by silence, the one sound he hadn't yet used. Thus there's no music, no beat.

> Miranda, dressed in black mourning clothes, delivered not a rap but what sounded like a poem; Hamilton's last flickers of thought and emotion were no longer tethered to a beat or a melody. "I wrote some notes for the beginning of a song someone will sing for me/America you great unfinished symphony/You sent for me," he said, quietly. Hamilton remembered his wife and friends, snatching at lyrical scraps from earlier songs as his coherence dissipated, the words forming a fractured, evanescent reprise, until he faltered and fell into silence. (Mead)

He flashes through all the events of his life, starting with the repeated deaths around him and "Burr, my first friend, my enemy." The ensemble dance around him in a memory of soldiers. As he wonders:

> Legacy. What is a legacy?
> It's planting seeds in a garden you never get to see
> I wrote some notes at the beginning of a song someone will sing for me
> America, you great unfinished symphony, you sent for me
> You let me make a difference

Eliza in her white gown slips past as he's on the turntable. All freezes and there's her loving pink light in the darkness – a single reason to live. However, he only bids her "take your time." He's resigned.

> [The Bullet] appears for a final time as the actual bullet, slowly approaching Hamilton throughout the entirety of his final monologue and coming dangerously close to him as he moves, scatter-brained, across the stage. Halfway

through, he steps right in her path, turns back and stumbles out of the way, and as he frantically repeats, "Rise up, rise up, rise up," she lunges for him, only to be pulled back by another ensemble member as Eliza steps in her path. Once Hamilton has been shot, she joins the ensemble once again, satisfied that the path she's been on since the beginning has come to an end. (Corde)

His final line, "Raise a glass to freedom!" salutes his dead friends in their tavern, the journey he embarked on in "My Shot" and the new country he helped build. It also visually resembles raising his pistol to the sky.

With this he delopes. He has faced violence and peace and chosen the latter. At the final moment, after hours of ambition, Hamilton deliberately throws away his shot...Burr doesn't. In *Drunk History,* Miranda notes that ordinarily Burr was cautious and Hamilton was reckless. But during this one duel, Burr hastily shot when Hamilton had no plans to fire at him. Meanwhile, Hamilton, always a lawyer, had carefully planned out the moment and left letters behind insisting he had no plans to shoot Burr – if he died, Burr was a treacherous villain.

In a red light, Burr shoots. Judge Pendleton, Hamilton's Second, reports, "The fire of Burr took effect, and Hamilton almost instantly fell. Burr then advanced toward Hamilton with a manner and gesture that appeared to be expressive of regret, but without speaking turned about and withdrew" ("The Duel").

As Angelica and Eliza bid their love goodbye, Burr reprises a bit of "Wait for It." There's a drum like a tense heartbeat and a clock chiming as time runs out and Burr sings bitterly that he's now a villain. Burr's actor says, "I think that our show is doing a really good job of reminding us that all of us are more than one thing" (*Hamilton's America*). Thus "Aaron Burr, Sir" and "The World Was Wide Enough" help Burr bookend the central plot.

Burr's line and song title that "The World was Wide Enough" alludes to a comment Burr made near the end of his life. He had two prized books – one, by the philosopher Voltaire, recommended a ruthless response to insults. The other was the popular comic novel *Tristam Shandy* by Lawrence Stern, in which a man is about to kill a fly, but stops, deciding the world is large enough for both of them. Burr said, "If I had read more Stern and less Voltaire, perhaps I would have realized that the world was large enough for both Hamilton and me" ("The Duel").

While defending oneself was gentlemanly, succeeding in killing one's opponent was considered savage, and Hamilton had been popular. Burr was one of the first duelists charged with murder. To avoid prosecution, he fled New York, leaving behind his mansion and all his possessions. After, he led a foolhardy attempt to invade Mexico, was tried for treason, and was forced into exile in Europe. His political career was destroyed (Isenberg 380).

Hamilton survived for thirty-one agonizing hours. He died on July 12, 1804, at age forty-nine. His sudden passing shocked the nation – the New York Supreme Court and Bank of New York draped black banners. For an entire month, New Yorkers wore black armbands (Chernow 710). New York City held the largest funeral in its history. Chernow concludes:

> There was a tremendous outpouring of grief and emotion. The funeral cortege went on for hours. I think literally every person in the city was lining the streets, looking out of windows, standing on roofs. It was said that every woman in particular was crying at the time of Hamilton's death. (*Alexander Hamilton: American Experience*)

He was buried behind Trinity Church in New York City, steps away from the site of the Treasury Office. Around the corner is Wall Street and the Stock Exchange he helped create.

Washington, all in white and lit up, enters and shares his friend's legacy. "Who lives, who dies, who tells your story," the ensemble sings. "The song is set to a reflective yet dramatic instrumental as Hamilton's friends and family close the play" ("Going H.A.M.").

Politicians speak of the effect Hamilton had on them. At last, his new biographer appears – Eliza. In her white gown and pink light, suggesting romance and a ghostly timeless purity, she interviews those who knew Hamilton and she speaks about him publically. "I put myself back in the narrative," she adds. During her fifty years that remained, she "established the first private orphanage in New York City" and campaigned to help build the Washington Monument.

"Eliza Hamilton tried to erase herself from her husband's story," keeping her own life private and commissioning books on her husband to celebrate his more public achievements (Chernow 728). Nonetheless, Chernow has restored her reputation, adding in his biography, "She was a woman of towering strength and integrity who consecrated much of her extended widowhood to serving widows, orphans, and poor children" (728). He writes a frame story, with the doughty widow at beginning and end. Miranda's character takes this a step still further and defiantly chooses to put herself in the narrative and become the new narrator.

She was buried at the foot of Hamilton's monument, while Angelica lies nearby in Trinity Church. Miranda describes the terrible sadness of "Angelica, near Alexander but not with him, for eternity" (*Hamilton: The Revolution* 281).

Onstage, Eliza sings about seeing him again until Hamilton arrives to take her hand and escort her for a moment, whirling in their ever-present cycle. She gasps in her pink light, suggesting she has found her Hamilton again even as she dies. Thus their story ends.

An alternate theory is that Eliza's gasp comes as the fourth wall falls and she beholds the audience, discovering that the story she's telling really does matter to history – she has succeeded in her final mission. In this case, the figure escorting her might not be Hamilton but the show's creator Lin-Manuel Miranda, revealing to her the audience she's earned.

VALERIE ESTELLE FRANKEL

LOOKING DEEPER:
HAMILTON
IMPACTS SOCIETY

The Creator

I am not throwing away my shot
I am not throwing away my shot
Hey yo, I'm just like my country
I'm young, scrappy and hungry
And. I'm not throwing away my shot.

"And if that sounds very much like the promise of a young playwright to himself, a goad to ambition and purpose, it should. There's as much Hamilton in Miranda as there is Miranda in Hamilton" (MagGregor). Indeed, *Hamilton* is the story of Lin-Manuel Miranda and his family. As the creator reveals: "My father came here the same age as Hamilton...he came with a full ride for NYU post-doc...didn't speak English" ("Hamilton: A Founding Father").

> When the composer, lyricist, and performer Lin-Manuel Miranda went on vacation in Mexico some seven years ago, he took Chernow's tome as a beach read. A couple of chapters in, reading about Hamilton as a "poor boy from the West Indies [who] commanded attention with the force and fervor of his words," Miranda saw—and more important, heard—the bragging, swaggering, word-spinning, quick-tempered men of the American Revolution synchronize with the hip-hop rhythms and run-ins that formed the popular sound track of his teen and early adult years. (Miranda was born in 1980.) Soon he was working on a mixtape that mashed up the founding fathers with beat-boxing bruthas. (Solomon)

As Miranda adds:

> The moment that cemented it was reading about how Hamilton's writing an essay gets him off the island [St. Croix]. It wasn't circumstance. He didn't stow away. He wrote an essay about how shitty the island was after a hurricane had destroyed it, and the essay became popular,

105

and he got a scholarship to get off the island because of that. I was like, "Oh, he literally wrote his way out of his circumstances. That's it! That's everything." (Binelli)

To him this was "Jay Z, Eminem, Biggie. Lil Wayne writing about Katrina! And so, having had that insight very early while reading Ron Chernow's book, I never pictured the literal Founding Fathers again" (Binelli).

It makes sense that he recast the Founding Fathers as Black and Latino – they look like himself and his fellow actors from *In the Heights.* "This is the story of America then told by America now. It looks like America now," Miranda explains ("Hamilton: A Founding Father"). As he adds:

I fell in love with Chernow's version of Hamilton. I recognized the relentlessness. I recognized the self-destructiveness. I recognize the "no one in the room's realized it yet, but I'm the smartest guy in here" of Hamilton, that energy. I went to a gifted school and I know that kid. And so I fell in love with his version of history, and seeing American history through his eyes made me see it in a totally different way. (Evans)

Many themes like Hamilton filling the world with words also reflect Miranda. "He was always very verbal. He read by 3, 3½," his father, Luis, tells. "We sent him to a local nursery school at 4 and he was the only reader, so he would read to the other kids, and the other kids would sort of be around him, because he was the one who could pick up a book" (MagGregor). There's also the "running out of time" motif. As he explains it:

I'm very aware that an asteroid could kill us all tomorrow. But I create works of art that take years and years to finish [laughs]. So it's an enormous act of faith to start a project. I think compounding that is my awareness that we lost Jonathan Larson before he ever got to see a preview of his show, *Rent.* He never saw what would change so many lives, mine included. So that sense of mortality is with me, always. ... So in that way, I'm very Hamilton-esque, in that I'm aware of both time and of the incredible opportunity that

I'm lucky to have, and not wanting to squander either.
(Binelli)

Like Hamilton, losing people early on made Miranda hyper-aware of death even as he writes defiantly in spite of his knowledge.

When he was four years old, a friend his age drowned in an accident. "I remember my parents telling me," Miranda says, dark eyes going darker. "I remember the ride to school that day because she used to ride with us. And she wasn't there. And I also remember sort of a year of gray." He became aware of his mortality freakishly early. "I imagine death so much it feels more like a memory," he raps as Hamilton, in a line he acknowledges as deeply autobiographical. "When is it gonna get me?" (Hiatt)

"What I share with Hamilton," Miranda acknowledges, "is that I want to get as many of the ideas out of my head as possible in the time I have" (Hiatt).

Hamilton was known to pace and mutter to himself while composing his treatises, something also seen in Miranda, who generally walks the dog and sings or raps along with his own background music every time he gets an idea.

Miranda describes in his documentary *Hamilton's America* as he was finishing writing the musical how he needed to wrap up his project and meet the baby his wife was expecting – just like Hamilton in Yorktown. "We're in exactly the same place," he concludes. Biographer Thomas Fleming says of Hamilton:

Hamilton was in love with fame, there's no doubt about that. But his understanding of fame is totally different from our understanding of fame. To be famous now is to be well known by everybody in the world, you're a celebrity. But that wasn't true in the eighteenth century. Fame was an achievement that a man created in the course of his life. He had to do something remarkable, he had to found a country or an empire. (*Alexander Hamilton: American Experience*)

Miranda's accomplishments too are based on what he's

done, what he's written. He's had a slow start, appearing in many shows before this blockbuster. He raps in *How I Met Your Mother:* "Bedtime Stories" (2013) and played the troubled rapper Juan 'Alvie' Alvarez on several episodes of *House*, as well as playing the recurring Dr. Ruben Marcado in *Do No Harm*. He also appeared in *The Sopranos, Modern Family, Sex and the City, The Electric Company, and Sesame Street.*

More important to his musical theater career was his other show, first attempted in college:

> By the time he started commuting to Hunter College High School on 94th Street, he was writing and performing his own shows, casting, producing and directing.
>
> He graduated and went off to Wesleyan and began writing the musical that would become *In the Heights,* about his familiar streets and the people he saw every day. He graduated in 2002 and kept writing. He took a job teaching English at his high school, and made ends meet by writing campaign jingles for his father's clients.
>
> By 2005 he and his friends, including director Thomas Kail, another Wesleyan grad, were able to mount a workshop production. *In the Heights* opened off-Broadway in 2007 and moved to Broadway in early 2008. It's a salsa-inflected rap snapshot of a Dominican block in Washington Heights and the lives of its residents, the complexity of love and loss, and like *Hamilton,* it too is about outsider striving and ambition, about having a foot in both worlds, about being torn between home and high achievement and whatever comes next. About insecurity and purpose and achieving your own big dreams. (MaGgregor)

In The Heights received nine Drama Desk nominations and it won the award for outstanding ensemble performance, received the Lucille Lortel Award and Outer Critics Circle Award for best musical, received the Obie Award for outstanding music and lyrics, and received a Theater World Award for Outstanding Debut Performance. *In the Heights* was nominated for the 2009 Pulitzer Prize for Drama. When he won the Tony for original score, he stood out by rhyming his acceptance speech.

He mentions "*Hamilton* feels twice as autobiographical as

In the Heights does" though the latter is about Puerto Rican immigrants. "We kind of double down on the themes of *In the Heights* and kind of blow them up to grand scope. We're not going to tell the story of an immigrant neighborhood. We're gonna tell the story of the first American immigrant and the formation of our country" ("Hip-hop and History Blend").

More recently, Miranda composed the cantina music for *Star Wars: The Force Awakens* and wrote lyrics for the songs of *Moana*. As he explains:

> Writing music for Star Wars was amazing. J.J. Abrams was here and I offhandedly joked, "Hey, if you need cantina music..." And he said, "I do need cantina music!" So that sort of gave me incredible courage. Ask the thing you want to ask your hero while your hero is in front of you! Don't be a dick, don't be obnoxious. But also know that you may never get that opportunity again. (Binelli)

Continuing his rise, he was awarded a MacArthur "genius grant" on September 29, 2015. He and Hamilton share a singular ambition:

> God help and forgive me
> I wanna build
> Something that's gonna
> Outlive me ("The Room Where It Happens")

"Hamilton himself died before age 50, and the musical isn't really about him, at its core. It's about a kid from a Puerto Rican family who grew up in New York City and went on to win the Pulitzer Prize for Drama," one critic concludes (Berman). Indeed, it is. As he sings this section as Hamilton, it's clear his legacy, like the statesman's, will last.

As his father reveals, "But the other thing that was always remarkable about him is that he works great as part of a team" (MagGregor). Like Hamilton in politics, Miranda can take the concept of a musical and with a group of stalwart friends, build something amazing.

The Team

"The fun for me in collaboration is, one, working with other people just makes you smarter, that's proven," says Miranda. "And this is not a singular art form – it's 12 art forms smashed together. We elevate each other. And two, it's enormously gratifying because you can build things so much bigger than yourself." (MagGregor)

Almost no musical on Broadway has had the same person contribute idea, story, music, lyrics, and lead performer. Still, Miranda didn't do everything himself. There was also his "cabinet" – director Thomas Kail, choreographer Andy Blankenbuehler and Alex Lacamoire. Lac, as he's called, is music director, arranger, orchestrator, conductor, and keyboard player. He explains, "I feel like I have such a strong opinion about how I think something should sound. But also because I know what Lin is looking for. I feel like I know how I can execute his vision" (*Hamilton's America*).

One reviewer notes:

This may be the most collaborative business there is, so credit goes in equal measure to every part of the creative team, even if the profiles take the "solitary genius" approach. Kail; Alex Lacamoire, music director; Andy Blankenbuehler, choreographer – Miranda calls it "The Cabinet." It's all one thing. One brain. They all worked together on *In The Heights*. You see them at rehearsal, in the calm eye of the Broadway hurricane, working and working and reworking what already works. They gesture with their coffee cups to the lights, the wings, the turntable. Maybe try this, maybe trim that. Maybe coffee is the real genius.

"It's about making the best possible thing," Miranda says. (MagGregor)

Another collaborator is the author of the book *Alexander Hamilton* that inspired it all. Winner of the Pulitzer Prize and the National Book Award, Ron Chernow is one of America's great biographers, with definitive books on J. P. Morgan, John D. Rockefeller, and George Washington. Having read his biography, which rescued Hamilton from obscurity and defended his legacy, Miranda asked Chernow to be his history expert and check the show for accuracy (MagGregor). He has commented on the script and staged version through their growth and frequent transformations. Meanwhile, Miranda was allowed a great deal of autonomy and he claimed it, telling the story he desired. He explains:

> What I appreciate about the theater business is that when I get in the room to talk about the content of the show with my producers and investors, I sit down with Oskar Eustis, who is the artistic director of The Public Theater; producer Jeffrey Seller, who brought *Rent* and *Avenue Q* to Broadway and co-produced *In the Heights*; and Tommy Kail, our director. Those are the people who make decisions and give me notes. Groundbreaking is what they do, so I never got a note saying, "Can they rap less?" or a visit from a cartoon cigar-chomping executive saying, "There's not a tune you can hum!" (DiGiacomo)

The musical's constant early changes likely result from Miranda's closeness with his showmates – often his old friends and always his fellow performers. Through the musical's creation, Miranda wrote lines inspired by his actors. When Miranda heard the Schuyler Sisters actresses singing R & B songs in their dressing room, he rewrote their first song to better showcase their harmonies (Miranda *Hamilton: The Revolution* 175). "We are influencing the piece by just being who we are" says Jasmine Cephas Jones (Maria) proudly.

Miranda comments, "I love when that happens as a writer – when you've got your head around the character and the actor who's going to be playing them, so you begin to write to their strengths. It happened to me with Chris Jackson [Washington] very early" (Evans). He adds, "And there was no one questioning casting decisions because the demands of this show are so specific that just finding someone with the right skill set seriously limited the talent pool" (DiGiacomo).

For Lafayette's rap, Miranda notes, "Doesn't hurt that Daveed [Diggs] is one of the most technically gifted rappers

I've ever met, so I knew I could built him tapestries" (*Hamilton: The Revolution* 119). He adds that lines like "'That's what I'm talkin about' are in because Anthony Ramos [Laurens/Phillip] says this all the time (*Hamilton: The Revolution* 80).

> Christopher Jackson, Hamilton's towering George Washington, has known Miranda the longest of any of the major cast members, having previously starred in *In the Heights*. "Lin told me about his idea for Hamilton a few days after that fateful vacation," Jackson recalls. "We were actually onstage doing *Heights*. He said, 'I've got the next thing. It's about the Treasury secretary!' And then he paused, and before I could say, 'What?!' the music started and we had to do '96,000.' When Ron Chernow came to see *Heights*, I had never seen Lin that nervous. He said, 'Ron Chernow's here!' I said, 'What does that mean?' And he said, 'The show needs to go well today.'"
> [Leslie Odom, Jr. (Burr)] first saw a workshop version of *Hamilton* at Vassar and found himself responding, almost viscerally, to "The Story of Tonight," an early number in which Hamilton and three friends (Mulligan, the Marquis de Lafayette and John Laurens) boisterously drink together in a tavern on the eve of the Revolution. "That's the one that made me a puddle, because it was four men of color onstage singing a song about friendship and brotherhood and love, and I had never seen that in a musical," Odom says. "I had seen white guys do it, in *Jersey Boys*, in *Les Mis*. Never seen a black guy. So I was a mess, and from that point, I was along for the ride." (Binelli)

The team made the characters their own, as creators inspired actors and actors inspired creators. Even as the current actors move on, their legacy remains in the lyrics devoted to them.

Themes and Motifs

Being satisfied versus ambitious is a major theme for Hamilton who always demands more from the world. As Eliza sings in "That Would Be Enough":

Look at where you are
Look at where you started
The fact that you're alive is a miracle
Just stay alive, that would be enough

The two motifs return after "The Reynolds Pamphlet," as Hamilton has alienated both women. Meanwhile, Angelica observes that Hamilton will never be satisfied. It takes a different, calmer personality – Eliza – to show being happy with what she already has, even as Hamilton is pursuing an affair. To Hamilton's surprise, Washington admits his own satisfaction and resigns the presidency. Hamilton finally offers, "That would be enough" in "It's Quiet Uptown," after all that he's lost. He returns Eliza's long-offered faith and trust by flipping her line, "I'm not afraid/I know who I married." Meanwhile, quiet, sweet Eliza lives for fifty years more and finds new ambitious projects like starting an orphanage…so many projects that she seems to have developed her husband's ambition and declares of her time, "It's not enough."

Also connected with ambition is all the rising and falling. There are cries of "Rise up!" (both rebelling and counter-pointing Hamilton's dreams of advancement) in "My Shot." "Raise a glass to freedom" has similar imagery. Contrasting this, Hamilton asks Burr: "If you stand for nothing, Burr, what do you fall for?" in "Aaron Burr, Sir" and "The Room Where It Happens." Burr is thus subtly compared to Lucifer, standing among all the Founding Father angels but ostracized and mistreated until he proudly rebels. "Wait for It" has him considering how success and failure both come to "the sinners and the saints" indiscriminately, thus pushing him towards nihilism and revenge. As Act I ends, Hamilton has completed his "rise to the top" but Burr warns him that his pride goeth before the fall, an arc that indeed occurs. The spinning turntable echoes the rise and fall, emphasizing its constant motion. His final "Rise up, rise up!" may even suggest heaven, as his friends look down from above. Alexander sees himself rise just before he falls to Burr's shot, suggesting this final battle has made him immortally beloved as a martyr with Burr the condemned villain. Symbolically, he has risen at last and Burr has forever tumbled.

Hamilton tells Burr and Lafayette, "I'll see you on the other side" in Act I, emphasizing the war as a great divide, followed by this line in his death scene – the greatest "other side." The first number emphasizes the deaths that have already set him on his path – his mother's, his cousin's. Hamilton also sings "I may not live to see our glory" in "The Story of Tonight," prophetically. "I imagine death so much it feels more like a memory/When's it gonna get me?" he wonders as early as "My Shot" before he decides to join the Revolution, setting up another phrase that will echo through the show and reminds the audience of his inevitable fate. As Miranda adds, "In this verse he goes from nihilism to a list of what needs to be done to hope towards tomorrow, and he takes himself there through one uninterrupted train of thought" (*Hamilton: The Revolution* 27). He repeats the first half of this in "Yorktown" and as he dies, emphasizing his many brushes with mortality.

On the concept of "Who lives, who dies, who tells our story," Miranda explains, channeling Shakespeare, "We strut and fret our hour upon the stage, and how that reverberates is entirely out of our control and entirely in the hands of those who survive us" (*Hamilton: The Revolution* 120). Legacy thus becomes central – Washington fusses over his history judges him before Yorktown and when he resigns, and Burr mourns that he's made himself the villain. "The Story of Tonight" has similar echoes. Hamilton craves "Something that's gonna/Outlive me" in "The Room Where It Happens," while Eliza insists they "don't need a legacy" in "That Would Be Enough." At the beginning of "The Room Where It Happens," Burr and Hamilton discuss General Mercer, whose death has gotten him a permanent legacy as a street in New York. Meanwhile, Eliza the biographer puts herself back into the story and redeems Hamilton by proudly sharing his papers and insights with the world. Thus she becomes the true savior. Rags to riches and the self-made hero become a major theme, introduced in line one. Tied in here is a theme of determination, relentlessness, seizing the moment, not throwing away one's shot. The beloved line "Immigrants! We get the job done" nods to America as the land of opportunity, even for outsiders. "Rise up" is a repeated line through the show, referencing revolution but also promotion. Meanwhile, privileged, puzzled Burr cannot comprehend the energy of the "bastard, orphan, son of a whore and a Scotsman," in a rap pattern he returns to throughout his narration. The final duel dramatically reverses roles – Hamilton throws away his shot while Burr seizes it.

The pair's rivalry is obviously another motif as they go from friends to rivals to deadly enemies through the arc. They frequently bump into each other face to face and each time repeat the same pattern, starting their conversation with "Aaron Burr, Sir," (or variants on this) and comparing how their life philosophies are going for them. By the end, Hamilton has tried Burr's "talk less" strategy to compromise with Jefferson, and Burr has started actively campaigning for president. Thus, as with *Wicked*, their friendship and rivalry has taught each to absorb qualities of the other.

Beyond this, there's an emphasis on genuine friendship, as the team of Laurens, Mulligan, and Lafayette welcome Hamilton and they bond as soldiers. Washington and Hamilton form such a tight connection that Hamilton follows him from aide-de-camp to Secretary of the Treasury (a parallel with Washington's Broadway actor, who followed Miranda from *In the Heights*). Angelica sets aside her romantic love for Hamilton to be an adoring sister to her and Eliza, a quick-witted confidante for them both until she finally picks sides in "The Reynolds Pamphlet." Thus sisterly love gets a nod, as does the brotherly love of Hamilton-Laurens and paternal love of Hamilton-Washington. Even the orphan finds a family.

There's romance of course, as Hamilton and Eliza's love

starts idealized (their eyes meet across the ballroom and they're engaged in weeks), complicated by Angelica and Maria in their love triangle and made worse as Hamilton abandons Eliza for his ambition. As the pair riff on "That Would Be Enough," they find a balance, but only after tragedy.

Waiting appears a great deal, from Hamilton's challenging repeated line "Just you wait" to Burr's much more guarded "Wait for it." The chord progression for the latter appears in "Aaron, Burr, Sir" and "The Story of Tonight" before Burr's show-stopping number. Meanwhile, in "The Room Where it Happens," Hamilton snarks on this philosophy, noting of governing, "You get love for it, you get hate for it/You get nothing if you wait for it." Eliza waits at home, the country waits to see who's won at Yorktown. Finally, the country is waiting through the Second Act for all the political changes as Washington's cabinet builds the US government from nothing.

Time and how much each person gets certainly echoes through the show. Hamilton writes "like you're running out of time," beginning with all the bustle of forging a new nation – when the line appears in "Best of Wives, Best of Women" he actually is. Framing the story with knowledge of his death at the beginning emphasizes how little he has. In his death scene, he adds, "I'm running out of time. I'm running and my time's up…" A clock chimes and all is silence.

A smaller motif is the string of chess metaphors. In Act I, they're associated with the war and include "Knight takes rook, but look" and "We snatch a stalemate from the jaws of defeat." In Act II, they're more political intrigue with "The pieces that are sacrificed in every game of chess" and "A game of chess, where France is queen- and kingless." Thus the literal battle becomes a figurative one, but Hamilton never stops strategizing.

"The world will never be the same," the ensemble sing in "Yorktown," and Angelica twists and echoes this in "Satisfied" to show how she's been transformed romantically. Thus the small scale mirrors the large one. The line also appears in "Guns and Ships" as Lafayette transforms the American army. As Burr sings it before shooting Hamilton, he cements the concept that a single death can be as transformative as the entire war. In fact, cycles are a strong motif in the story, as the American Revolution sparks the French one, and election follows election. The swirling turntable, as with the *Les Mis* song "Turning, Turning," emphasizes progression through time as the same battles must be fought over and over. It spins as Hamilton flings himself into years of writing, or as he's caught in the hurricane of his childhood that mirrors his mother's death and his present political helplessness. Set designer David Korins liked the cinematic aspects of the circular concept:

> It's a sweeping epic, storytelling tool and the show is so epic in scale that when I pitched it to the director and the choreographer, I actually wrote out several different beats of the show where I imagined we could use this kind of swirling movement. You can also use it like a treadmill; there are many applications of this thing. This swirling movement is really important to the storytelling. (Eddy)

Hamilton and Politics

> If every presidential administration gets at least one mass-cultural moment it deserves, then Hamilton has become the Obama era's *Wall Street*, its *24*, its *Spice World* – even more so, perhaps, because the show has actually managed to fulfill candidate Obama's promise to bridge the divide between Red and Blue America. Fans of Hamilton include Mitt Romney, Hillary Clinton, Bernie Sanders, Dick Cheney and the president himself. (Binelli)

Obama is a great fan and saw the show several times. He says of it, "Part of what's so powerful about this performance is it reminds us of the vital, crazy kinetic energy that's at the heart of America – that people who have a vision and a set of ideals can transform the world" (*Hamilton: The Revolution* 284). Thus he linked it with the drive and passion of the modern country. As he added on another occasion:

> And in the Hamilton that Lin-Manuel and his incredible cast and crew bring to life—a man who is "just like his country, young, scrappy, and hungry"—[laughter]—we recognize the improbable story of America and the spirit that has sustained our Nation for over 240 years. Now, in this telling, rap is the language of revolution. Hip-hop is the backbeat. In each brilliantly crafted song, we hear the debates that shaped our Nation, and we hear the debates that are still shaping our Nation. We feel the fierce, youthful energy that animated the men and women of Hamilton's generation. And with a cast as diverse as America itself, including the outstandingly talented women, the show reminds us that this Nation was built by more than just a few great men and that it is an inheritance that belongs to all of us. (Obama)

Miranda responds that writing the show has given him new realizations about the presidency.

> You know, the thing I think about when Cheney comes, Clinton comes, all these guys, I always think of the song "History Has Its Eyes on You." Because these guys are graded on such a harsh curve, man. Like, Jefferson right now is being re-litigated because he's a character in this show. That was a long time ago! I got to ask the president about that, when we visited the White House last time. I said, "What do you think about the fact that you're going to be in textbooks 200 years from now? How do you pick up a pen in the morning? How do you get out of bed?" Because I couldn't handle that shit.
> What did he say?
> He said, "It's freeing, actually." Which I found really interesting. I said, "Why?" And he said, "Because I could be unpopular today, and that's OK. I can tell myself, 'All right, people who loved me are really mad at me today, but I think I did something that will make life incrementally better a generation or two generations from now.' And I'm OK with being unpopular because I know I'm being graded on a crazy, longer curve." (Binelli)

Miranda started writing this show in 2009, as the modern-day Tea Party movement was taking off. He comments:

Well, specifically, having the Founding Fathers look like America today strikes me as so radical. And it made me think of some of the Tea Party rhetoric, of how these conservatives were saying, "We need to take our country back." And to me, this show felt like it was saying, "No, you're not taking the country back, and in fact, we're part of the whole history of this country, even going back to the puffy shirts and the tricorn hats."

I guess the direct line I can pull on the most is between Hamilton's life story and the immigrant narrative in our country. The fact that immigrants have to work twice as hard just to get here, but that also, at some point, it's going to be thrown in your face as a negative. In Hamilton's case, it was Jefferson and Madison writing basically the same things you would hear about Obama during election cycles: "How do we really know where he's from?"

Right. (Binelli)

The show provoked thought about race, class, and political cowardice – issues still apparent today in our debates. Who should get to be the president? How many has gun violence harmed in its frivolous attempts to prove men's courage? There's something for everyone in the story:

Conservatives can revel in Hamilton's role in creating American capitalism, with its credit system, banking, and stock market (never mind his insistence on checks and balances, including regulations, taxation, and the strong federal government that he favored over states' rights, and his rejection of American exceptionalism); they can cheer on Jefferson as a denouncer of big government and exponent of individual liberties (never mind his rank dishonesty, lack of scruples, and defense of slave-owning). ...Like many musicals before it, Hamilton offers an appealing wish for a mythic idea: in this case, as Hamilton sings toward the end, a vision of America as "a place where even orphan immigrants can leave their fingerprints and / rise up." This still happens, of course, but if Hamilton had been sent here today to attend college as he was some 240 years ago, he'd have accrued a huge burden of student-loan debt and would have been kicked back to the Caribbean as soon as his student visa expired. (Solomon)

119

The first Republican Presidential debate for the 2016 presidential campaign aired during Hamilton's opening night, and from then on the show remained tied to the Donald Trump/Hillary Clinton presidential election of 2016. Trump was proclaiming he would build a wall and keep immigrants out, while Hillary wanted to naturalize them. "While Bobby Jindal declared that "immigration without assimilation is invasion," an opening night audience watched a musical about the Founding Fathers that rests on an ideal explicitly stated in the first act: "Immigrants/We get the job done" (James). Miranda adds:

> The fights we're having right now politically are the same fights we've been having since six months after we became a country: states' rights versus national rights, foreign intervention versus how we treat our own people and the rights we have. The original sin of slavery and its repercussions; the original sins of, "Oh shit, we said everyone could have guns and now everyone has guns" — that's all still here and we're going to be reckoning with it all as long as we're a country. It's *MSNBC* and *Fox News* instead of Hamilton and Jefferson, and the polarities have flipped several times, but we're always going to be having these struggles. We will have periods of anger, and we will have periods of bloodshed, but hopefully we'll take more steps forward than we take back. (DiGiacomo)

On Clinton versus Trump, Miranda said in an interview, that he wouldn't dream of taking sides publically. "I would rather play the back half of a horse in *Equus* [laughs]. I always get involved in voter drives. But I have no desire for my Twitter feed to be filled with a bunch of people screaming ad hominem attacks against anyone who voiced something different from how they feel. I don't feel the need to get in the middle of that."

He added that blaming immigrants (Trump's platform) has always been part of America, from "Irish Need Not Apply" to Buchanan in the Nineties (Binelli). As he commented:

It would be fun to have Donald Trump see the show. I'd be interested to see his reactions to the fact that one of our greatest commanders of the Revolutionary War and the creator of the financial system that allowed his father to get rich and allowed him to play with his father's money were both immigrants. (DiGiacomo)

When he hosted *Saturday Night Live*, he riffed humorously on the politics of his own show. "It's such a nice escape from all the craziness in our world right now. It's about two famous New York politicians locked in a dirty ugly mud-slinging political campaign – escapism!" In his parody, he barely escaped calling Trump (at the time campaigning for president) a piece of sh—" He concluded, "And as long as I remember/to vote this November/I am not throwing away my shot," reminding fans to vote. ("Lin-Manuel Miranda Monologue – SNL").

With some exceptions, the younger, ethnically diverse crowd who loved *Hamilton* saw presidential candidate Donald Trump as the opposition – the King of England dragging the people back to medieval times as Trump questioned women's rights and climate change. On campaign, he blamed immigrants for taking American jobs, promised to build a wall between the US and Mexico, and was actually endorsed by the KKK and Neo-Nazi groups.

Thus many fans picked up on election and *Hamilton* parallels. "You'll Be Trumped" fits many of Trump's campaign promises to the king's song. "The Schyuler Sisters" song is spoofed in the song "The Trump Wives (a Hamilton parody)." Their "Look around, look around, at how scary it is to be alive right now" is pointedly disturbing. Bernie Sanders gets an "Alexander Hamilton" crossover too. *The Epic Rap Battles of History* version may not precisely be a Hamilton parody, but it certainly feels like it as it reimagines the debates. "Hamiltrump" covers the election, rewriting "Alexander Hamilton," to spoof many of Trump's top quotes. The Key of Awesome's "Hamilton Parody" takes on the same song. It features many well-acted celebrities with excellent voice impressions (and Michelle Obama slaps Bill Clinton who admits "I deserved that"). More and more parodies continue: Trumpleton: The Musical's "Ted Cruz, Loser" (off "Aaron Burr, Sir"), Tyler Davis's "Donald Trump ('Alexander Hamilton' Parody)," "Media on Your Side," "Farmer Refuted (240 Years Later)," Nerd Squad's "TRUMP: An Anti-American Musical," Ingrid Windsland's "I Know Him (Trump Parody)" and an entire series by Randy Rainbow.

Only a week after the polarizing election, perhaps the most emotional in history, politics burst onto the *Hamilton* stage. Vice President-elect Mike Pence, who had once passed harsh anti-gay legislation, and was serving beside the man insisting he would build a wall across the Mexican border to keep people out, attended the show. Aware of the contradictions of this man watching a Broadway show, some in the crowd booed the Vice President-elect, or cheered extra-long at "Immigrants/We get the job done!" At the end, the cast, all of whom had gay or immigrant friends or family, felt driven to address him. Brandon Dixon, who played Aaron Burr, began the short prepared statement by thanking Pence for attending the play and saying, "We hope you will hear us out."

> "We, sir – we are the diverse America who are alarmed and anxious that your new administration will not protect us, our planet, our children, our parents, or defend us and uphold our inalienable rights," Dixon said. "We truly hope that this show has inspired you to uphold our American values and to work on behalf of all of us." (Bradner)

That night, Trump angrily sent tweets such as "The Theater must always be a safe and special place. The cast of Hamilton was very rude last night to a very good man, Mike Pence. Apologize!" which earned some eye-rolling from the public (Bradner). As some posted on social media that they would boycott the show, others eagerly offered to take their tickets (though few of either set of posters were actually in

New York).

Meanwhile, in the midst of this flurry, Pence announced he wasn't offended. "My daughter and I and her cousins really enjoyed the show. *Hamilton* is just an incredible production, incredibly talented people. It was a real joy to be there," he said. "When we arrived we heard a few boos, and we heard some cheers," he said, "I nudged my kids and reminded them that is what freedom sounds like" (Bradner). Finally, on *The Late Show with Stephen Colbert*, after the Pence visit, Colbert protested that the musical was not "overrated" as "It has finally given old white people a way to enjoy rap!" Colbert then donned a blond wig and tricorn and spoofed "Alexander Hamilton" for a short Trump rap of his own.

In its themes, the show offers many more protests to issues of 2016:

This is part musical, part protest music; characters rap their way through songs with themes and lines that wouldn't be entirely out of place at a Black Lives Matter protest (*"and though I'll never be truly free / until those in bondage got the same rights as you and me"*) or a Bernie Sanders rally (*"They tax us unrelentlessly / Then King George turns around and has a spending spree"*). Both lyrics come from "My Shot," a song that turns into a rallying cry for protest and revolution: *"Rise up / when you're living on your knees / you rise up / tell your brother that he's gotta / rise up / tell you sister that she's gotta / rise up."* In 2015, it was hard for me to watch so many brown bodies play this scene out onstage and not immediately think of the images that came out of Ferguson.

If Alexander Hamilton is the show's protester/agitator, then Aaron Burr — with his advice of *"talk less / smile more"* — is the show's Respectability Politic. Burr's lines are quieter, more spoken word than the driving raps performed by Hamilton and the other revolutionaries like Lafayette, Hannibal, and Laurens. In "Farmer Refuted," Hamilton shouts down the Tory representative Seabury rather like Marissa Johnson and Mara Willaford with Bernie Sanders in Seattle, while Burr urges *"let him be."* Burr's philosophy is mapped out perfectly here: *"Geniuses, lower your voices / You keep out of trouble and you double your choices / I'm with you but the situation is fraught / You've got to be carefully taught / If you talk you're gonna get shot.*" It's a "you catch more flies with honey than vinegar" strategy that mirrors accusations from GOP candidates like Ben Carson that the Black Lives Matter movement is too "divisive." But it's the urgency to force change – the kind of urgency that has prompted the BLM protests, and interrupted presidential campaign stops, and inspired constant chatter on social media platforms – that Miranda captures perfectly at the end of Act 1 in "Non-Stop." (James)

"The U.N. Security Council came to see the show at the Public," Miranda remembers one afternoon, "and our U.S. ambassador said, 'There are so many world leaders I would love to bring to the show just to show them George Washington stepping down – because the story of history is leaders leading on populism, then not leaving'" (MagGregor). Further, there's a message about the helplessness and dissatisfaction of the governed as leaders make the big decisions:

> COMPANY: We want our leaders to save the day—
> BURR: But we don't get a say in what they trade away
> COMPANY: We dream of a brand new start—
> BURR: But we dream in the dark for the most part ("The Room Where It Happens")

The rap battle in the show between Jefferson and Hamilton about some states having to bail out other states is still an issue today in America, as is the question of their second battle – should America intervene in foreign wars? Sometimes there's a lot of audience reaction to "If we try to fight in every revolution in the world, we never stop." Miguel Cervantes, who will star as Hamilton when the show opens in Chicago in September 2016 concludes:

> That phrase—"history is happening"—could not be more true now politically, socially, [and] environmentally. We are in just as much turmoil in our country now as they were then. Everything is changing. It will be a time [to which] people will look back and say, "Look at what happened." I

really hope we're as successful as our buddy Alexander
Hamilton when future generations look back to this time.
(Kowalski)

Hamilton and Pop Culture

Jeffery Seller, the producer, notes, "I have never in my
life seen a musical that has penetrated the American culture
faster than Hamilton" (*Hamilton's America*). Miranda
comments, "That's the fun of this story, too, is that it is sort
of a love letter to New York and the things that happened
here. It's always been this hub for creation" (Evans). Events
take place all over the city in residences that once belonged to
Jefferson, Burr, and Hamilton.

Of course, Broadway has often spun off live parodies and
mash-ups. *Spamilton*, the parody of the musical, played at The
Triad on W 72nd St in New York City. On *YouTube*, the
Maccabeats parody the musical with new lyrics to the songs
in "Hasmonean - A Hamilton Hanukkah." Their King
George number fits particularly well. Continuing the
crossovers, people have used the tune of "Alexander
Hamilton" to retell plucky origin stories of Rudolph the
Reindeer, Jesus, Sir Isaac Newton, Harry Potter, Daenerys
Targaryen, The Chicago Cubs, Luke Skywalker, Steven
Universe, and Batman of all things on *YouTube* videos.
There's a Cap vs Iron Man rap battle and the songs "My
Spock" and "Dumbledore on Your Side" too. "You'll Be
Back" is likely the second most popular spoof song, mashed
up with *The Legend of Zelda, Dragonball Z, Harry Potter, Underfell,*
and *The Phantom of the Opera*. The Schuyler Sisters are
reimagined as Disney Princesses, *Star Wars* heroines, and the
sisters from *Hocus Pocus*. The Lamplighters also spoofed the
musical. Burr's actor Leslie Odom, Jr. reenacted the Hamilton
vs Burr "Got Milk?" commercial as an ad for the musical.

"The 2016 Song- A Year in Review" emphasizes all the
problems with 2016 – all the political and environmental
disasters, all narrated by Tessa Netting to "Alexander
Hamilton" as she hits all the pop culture moments of the

VALERIE ESTELLE FRANKEL

year. "This new year you must do what you can," the song concludes. Finally, Conan did a parody on his show called "Camelton" with a live camel in a curled wig and cravat only to have Matthew Broderick protest that Hamilton spoofs had been done to death. After hearing his song, Brodrick admitted Conan had "improved on the original."

For pop culture moments, there's also the attendees:

Hamilton is basically the place for celebrity sightings. "All the celebrities come backstage after the show, and they're always nice – most of them are just flabbergasted by us," ensemble member Ariana DeBose says. "They either gush or they're speechless. I love both reactions, because it means we did our job." From Hollywood heavy-hitters to politicians, here's a sampling of the glitterati who've taken seats at the Richard Rodgers Theatre:

President Barack Obama and the First Family Jay Z and Beyoncé Oprah Winfrey Julianne Hough and Vanessa Hudgens (best girls' night out ever) Idina Menzel Meryl Streep Alan Cumming Lena Dunham Matthew McConaughey Neil Patrick Harris Cate Blanchett Lea Michele (whose BFF, Jonathan Groff, played the role of King George III) Amy Schumer Jennifer Lopez Julia Roberts Laverne Cox John Stamos (*Full House*'s Uncle Jesse!) Lupita Nyong'o Will Ferrell Julie Andrews Kanye West Daniel Radcliffe Debbie Allen Gloria Estefan Alicia Keys Jesse Tyler Ferguson Kristin Chenoweth Karlie Kloss Katy Perry Gloria Steinem (Feller)

More impacts on culture include the Obamas introducing the musical at the Tonys and Miranda guesting on *SNL* singing "My Shot" with adapted lyrics. He began by explaining that he wouldn't be singing from the show because appearing on *SNL* was a cherished opportunity. As he transitioned he rapped, "My name is Lin-Manuel, I am hosting *SNL,* and I am not throwing away my shot!" A parody ensued, in which he made plans for his guest appearance and rapped happily about appearing on their celebrity wall ("Lin-Manuel Miranda Monologue – SNL").

Miranda also did an episode of *Drunk History* on Burr and Hamilton. During her acceptance speech at the Democratic

126

National Convention, Hillary Clinton invoked *Hamilton* in saying "Let our legacy be about 'planting seeds in a garden you never get to see.'"

At the time of the musical, the ten-dollar bill came under scrutiny, with the White House staff considering putting a woman on a bill at last. However, the show's fandom quaffed the idea of it being the ten. "There's even the question of whether or when Hamilton will come off the $10 bill. While everyone agrees it's time for an American woman on our paper money, very few think the father of our paper money is the guy to replace. Better bloody, bloody Andrew Jackson, who killed a lot of folks – and sold many fewer tickets on Broadway," one critic protests (MagGregor).

> It's a rare example of theater penetrating deeply into mainstream culture. "Hamilton Trash"—as some high school fans call themselves—spread the gospel by referencing the show in elaborate senior-prom proposals and college-admission essays. In the adult world, *Hamilton* turned up in WikiLeaked Democratic National Committee emails, Hillary Clinton's nomination speech and Sarah Jessica Parker's Met Gala outfit. (Berman)

Miranda and the cast actively engage with fans on *Twitter* and *Instagram*, and their fans respond with fan art, vids, and reviews. "Beyoncé told Jonathan Groff, who played King George, that she's going to steal his moves. And rappers such as Common, Busta Rhymes and Talib Kweli have given it a hip-hop seal of approval in interviews" (Berman).

> A few anecdotal observations about the Hamilton-obsessed: They're on a first-name basis with cast members, even though they've likely never met. Upon hearing that I share his beloved wife's name, they sing it back to me, lingering on the swooning middle syllable a touch longer, as the ensemble does in the show's closing number. Many listen to the cast recording daily. Some Twitter-stalk its stars and use the voices of Phillipa Soo (Eliza Schuyler Hamilton) and Renée Elise Goldsberry (Angelica Schuyler) as their ringtones. More than once,

they have described levitating out of their seats during the show. (Berman)

As television shows reference it and news shows parody it, *Hamilton* has clearly made its impact.

Rewriting Racism and Sexism

To add to the cheek of casting himself as Hamilton, Miranda has cast black actors to play Washington, Jefferson, Madison, Lafayette, and Aaron Burr. But it isn't just cheek, or a way to make history seem contemporary and fresh": Miranda is knitting past and present together, reminding us that, say, the upper Manhattan neighborhood named after Washington is today strongly identified with its Latino population. In Miranda's view, the Founders, being revolutionaries, are misfits-grasping, rash, arrogant, foolhardy. It isn't such a stretch to say that their personalities overlap with those of today's blustering, cocky rappers, and Miranda's usage of contemporary musical idioms such as rap makes the story as contemporary and urgent as it was at the time it was happening. (Smith)

Miguel Cervantes, who starred as Hamilton when the show opened in Chicago in September 2016 said:

This is what our country looks like. It's a mix of all of these types of people. Regardless of what the men and women looked like 200 years ago, what the people look like now is this. What the music sounds like is this.

I think that's part of the magic of it—the storytelling aspect and the hip-hop style. The cultural diversity of the performers [reflects the diversity] of the people that you see singing those songs in pop culture.

[Our] George Washington ... doesn't look like the one on the $1 bill. That has an effect on how you think about history and how you think about how our country is now. (Kowalski)

Director Thomas Kail explains, "What we're trying to do with the cast and the larger gesture of the show is say here's a group of people that you think you can't relate to. Maybe we can take down some of those barriers and allow a reflection to be truer" (*Hamilton's America*). "The theatrical, corporeal point, which can't be conveyed by the script or score alone, is that America's history— and its future—belong to men and women of color as profoundly as to anyone else" (Solomon).

> There's an almost indescribable power in seeing the Founders, in an otherwise historically rigorous production, portrayed by a young, multiracial cast. "It is quite literally taking the history that someone has tried to exclude us from and reclaiming it," says Leslie Odom Jr., who comes close to stealing the show with his turn as Hamilton killer Aaron Burr. "We are saying we have the right to tell it too." (Binelli)

Lafayette comments, "Immigrants…" Then they finish the line in unison while high-fiving each other: "…we get the job done!" The audience always cheers. *Variety* wrote that "in the end, Miranda's impassioned narrative of one man's story becomes the collective narrative of a nation, a nation built by immigrants who occasionally need to be reminded where they came from" (Stasio). The country was built by immigrants, always bullied as outsiders and newcomers whatever their skin color. Alexander Hamilton was just one more, and his skin color in the show emphasizes that he could be an immigrant today.

Miranda says he's experienced prejudice in his own life "as often as any other Latino male growing up in the United States. So — often." (Hiatt). Several times, fellow attendees at black-tie events have assumed he was a waiter: "Even after *In the Heights* opened, I was at a thing and a lady waves me over and goes, 'She never got her salad.'" (Hiatt). He also describes the lack of parts for Latino men before he created many parts in *In The Heights* ("Hip-hop and History Blend"). As he adds:

> I can't say I have enough experience with Hollywood to feel that I've encountered racism there. I can tell you that I did about five fruitless years of auditioning for voiceovers where I did variations on tacos and Latin accents, and my first screen role was as a bellhop on *The Sopranos*. It was actually an amazing experience. James Gandolfini stayed and did his sides even though he wasn't onscreen. That's the mark of the kind of actor Gandolfini was.

> I don't differentiate between black and Latino actors.
> We're in the same struggle to be represented in a way
> that's even close to honest. And I can tell you that the
> amount of Latino characters I can point at and say, "That's
> what my life experience looks like" — I can't think of any off
> the top of my head besides Jimmy Smits in *Mi Familia*.
> (DiGiacomo)

Of course, only some of the country was built by immigrants – a significant amount was built by slaves.

While many who tell of the Founding Fathers don't dwell on the slavery issue, Miranda brings it into the text over and over, starting with the show's tenth line. Pro-slavery, elite Jefferson is one of the antagonists, and his slave mistress, Sally Hemings, gets a quick appearance. As Laurens actively campaigns for an end to slavery and Hamilton calls Jefferson out on who's really tilling his fields ("we all know who's really doing the planting," Hamilton spits during Act II), the musical confronts America's darkest shame. This current appears in the show:

> HAMILTON/LAURENS:
> We'll never be free until we end slavery!
>
> …
> LAURENS: Black and white soldiers wonder alike if this
> really means freedom
> WASHINGTON: Not. Yet ("Yorktown")

As the show ends, Washington bows his head, acknowledging his own culpability here, as Eliza regrets in the final number that Hamilton couldn't do everything he wanted, like end the torture and sale of fellow human beings.

Chernow explains: "Hamilton co-founds the first anti-slavery society in New York, The Manumission Society. He's arguably the most consistent abolitionist among the founders, and it's kind of a thread that runs consistently throughout his entire life" (*Alexander Hamilton: American Experience*). Historian Carol Berkin adds:

I think his opposition to slavery is of a piece with his general belief in meritocracy. He says slavery keeps men, who might make major contributions to our society – prevents them from doing that and so it's inefficient. It doesn't let people who have talent use their talents well. (*Alexander Hamilton: American Experience*)

Thus "Black Lives Matter" gets a voice in the show, reminding the audience how central the issue was in Hamilton's life. It's a quiet reflection on the many ways to uphold human dignity.

In "The Schuyler Sisters" Angelica and her sisters announce ideals quite anachronistic as they want to be included in equality. Angelica has also been reading politics and her sisters mirror her words:

ANGELICA: I've been reading *Common Sense* by Thomas Paine
So men say that I'm intense or I'm insane
You want a revolution? I want a revelation
So listen to my declaration:
ELIZA/ANGELICA/PEGGY: "We hold these truths to be self-evident
That all men are created equal"
ANGELICA: And when I meet Thomas Jefferson
I'm 'a compel him to include women in the sequel!

Whether or not women said this in the day (Abigail Adams, in fact, urged her husband to "remember the ladies" while creating their new country), they have a voice now in this uppity character.

Lorens tells both men and women to "rise up," adding the line "tell your sister," suggesting it's her revolution too. Historically a few women like Sarah Bishop went to war and others like Molly Pitcher loaded cannons. But housewives did contribute, donating their family pewter and their rooves for bullets.

Later, Burr campaigns, reminding women to "tell your husbands" – they did not have the vote, but they could thus influence the political process.

131

> And while the story of the founding fathers is a story about men, Miranda makes a real effort to give Angelica and Eliza Schuyler more agency and inner life than they are typically granted. Blankenbuehler also creates plenty of gender-neutral dancing. While conventions reign in scenes like the ball at which Hamilton meets the Schuyler sisters—which segues beautifully into Hamilton and Eliza's wedding, as seen through Angelica's eyes—in the battle sequences, men and women make up the battalions, and their putty-colored breeches and vests match, too. (Solomon)

Eliza is a gentle, retiring wife, happy to stay at home and raise the children. She spends the story urging Hamilton into domesticity. At the same time, Eliza sings to her husband: "Oh, let me be a part of the narrative/In the story they will write someday" ("That Would Be Enough"). She does not sing the traditional "torch song" of unrequited love as some heroines do – in the mood of "As Long As He Needs Me" from *Oliver!* and "On My Own" from *Les Miserables*. Instead, her solo song is one of quiet determined revenge against her husband in the one way she wants to hurt him – their shared words and legacy.

Still, she desires a place in history for herself, much like the one Hamilton is creating. Thus in this musical, she gets to be a part of the narrative in a story that's most often reserved for Martha Washington and Abigail Adams. She takes over the final song, describing her great deeds like building an orphanage and how she puts herself in the narrative once more.

Educational Strategies

Leslie Odom, Jr. says that as a black man he feels more invested in the country now that he's played a Founding Father, something he expects will expand to high schoolers when they get to do the play. "The empathy that requires, the connections you make, the lines you draw between the things you want and the things they wanted, that you love and they loved, I never found all that connective tissue before this show" (*Hamilton: The Revolution* 160). Students noted of the recast founding Fathers, "It just made me really proud, and feel good about being American. Like I belong here" (*Hamilton: The Revolution,* 159).

For school productions, there are 21 parts in the original show, ranging from tiny to enormous. In fact, students might split the double roles like Lafayette/Jefferson in half to allow more chances to star. There are far more male parts than female ones, but there's no reason some of the founding fathers couldn't be played by women in a further subversion of history. And of course this show offers lots of parts for young actors of color – often a gap in traditional musical theater.

Many critics joyfully consider the musical "a gateway drug that animates a passion to learn more about its subjects, and not just their foibles and personalities but their ideas" (Smith).

> Even when the lights dim on Hamilton, its core ideas will live on in schools. For teachers of history and social studies, Hamilton is manna from the curriculum gods, and the show has officially partnered with the nonprofit Gilder Lehrman Institute of American History and others to send students from select disadvantaged high schools to see the musical at a drastically reduced price, and develop accompanying study materials. "Finally, a medium to talk about history that is interesting to people under 18," says Brian Collier, a member of the graduate faculty at the University of Notre Dame's Institute for Educational Initiatives. In a teaching-methods course this summer, he had master's-degree candidates develop lesson plans using the musical—which he sees, in the best sense of the term, as a "gateway drug"—to teach academic skills. (Berman)

"With the current #EduHam initiative, allowing 20,000 high schoolers, most from low-income families, to see the show for $10 and perform their own raps onstage, Hamilton's educational potential seems limitless" (Matteson). Many students are rapping and composing on their own, and some are even reading the biography.

Brendan Bell, who teaches U.S. History, Government and Economics at Cristo Rey High School in Sacramento, sees the songs as the hook. "One thing that really speaks to my students is music, especially hip-hop," he says. "They're very perceptive to the messages within lyrics. They already bring up societal and institutional issues about peace, racism and civil rights, so I anticipate that they'll react [to Hamilton] with a lot of energy." (Berman). He's teaching a Hamilton-themed lesson asking "What is the American Dream?" and "What is the immigrant experience like across our history?" The musical, of course, allows him to connect the Founding Fathers with students' present-day experience.

> Deynika Joree attended a performance of Hamilton in April as part of the Gilder Lehrman Institute's educational program. For Joree, whose parents emigrated from Guyana, Hamilton was a revelation. "When I first heard about the show, I expected all these white actors and actresses, but when I started to realize the entire cast is completely diverse, people from all different backgrounds— brown, black, Hispanic—I was just like, 'This is good,'" says the senior at Thomas A. Edison Career and Technical Education High School in Queens. "Lin said that the reason he did that is to show America as it is now, and that was a really big thing for me." (Berman)

Another teacher posts lesson plans for teaching with "Farmer Refuted" and "You'll Be Back." She asks when art has inspired students to learn more, then describes how Miranda picked up Ron Chernow's biography and wrote the musical.

"What's striking about Hamilton is that between the story and the music, it has multiple entry points. Every student was engaged in a way that was meaningful to them" (Matteson). She then does a close reading of the two songs, having students annotate the text and then listen to the music as a class. Discussing tone, character, and clever wordplay, the students learn much about analysis. As she adds:

> In our close read of "Right Hand Man," students were charged with comparing the George Washington in the song with the legend they know. We considered how rap added to the emotion of the song. Finally, I challenged them to give Washington's rap a try. The rhythm and rhyme speak directly to the future president's state of mind, creating an empathy that we rarely feel for this legendary figure. I wanted my students to feel that—and respect the skill required to perform it. (Matteson)

Of course, most students don't live close to where Hamilton is being performed, and even if they do, it can be unfeasible to arrange a field trip. Still, along with the *Broadway Cast Recording*, the transcripts are online (at Genius.com and Lyricsondemand.com), and the PBS documentary *Hamilton's America* can provide well-filmed clips without the stigma of bootlegs. The school library can even buy and license a copy of the latter.

Other Musicals

In the second footnote on the first page of the libretto, Lin-Manuel explains that the opening number of *Hamilton* – initially a monologue for Aaron Burr and the first song written – "owes a debt to the prologue of *Sweeney Todd:* All our characters set the stage for our main man's entrance." In fact, in *Sweeney Todd*, the hero, now dead, rises from the grave to tell his own story as a flashback that lasts the entire musical, a structure that likewise inspired Miranda. Sweeney, with all his energy and justification for his behavior, *is* the show, much as Hamilton is. *Hamilton*'s opening number "sets the style, the tone (unique as it is) and the point of view of the show perfectly (complete with the information that the hero will be dead at the final blackout)" (Viertel 60).

Completing the frame, the citizens, joined by the ghosts of all the expired protagonists, recite "The Ballad of Sweeney Todd" at show's end. In *Hamilton*, Eliza soon takes over the final number. It's unusual to end a musical with someone other than the protagonist, but Miranda felt that another

135

musical, in this case, *Caroline or Change,* gave him permission (*Hamilton: The Revolution* 280).

Miranda admired Weidman for his history-musicals like *Pacific Overtures* and *Assassins.* He particularly asked how to winnow down history into just a few hours (*Hamilton: The Revolution* 173). Jack Viertel comments in his book *The Secret Life of the American Musical* that *Oklahoma!* questioned the American identity and the meaning of democracy, returning in many revivals but also inspiring more shows on this question. "From *Bloomer Girl* to *Hair* to *1776* to *Hairspray* to *Hamilton,* we keep wrestling with the questions raised by Rogers and Hammerstein's first hit" (10).

At the same time, Miranda adored the witch's rap in *Into the Woods* with its heavy backstory turned into entertainment, and echoes of this appear in the exposition-heavy raps. Building on this, "My Shot" is the "I want" song – echoed in "Wouldn't It Be Loverly?" from *My Fair Lady* and "Some People" from *Gypsy.* Viertel calls "My Shot" "a distant but recognizable descendant" of *West Side Story*'s "Something's Coming" as the hero seeks a better life (59).

There are several more steps he details such as "the conditional love song," as in, "If I Loved You" from *Carousel* or "I'll Know" from *Guys and Dolls.* This is seen in "Helpless," of course, but even more in Angelica's skeptical "Satisfied." Eliza succumbs but Angelica holds back, to the point of losing Hamilton to her sister.

With this many influences (to say nothing of the history books!) the sources for the show are mind-boggling. At the same time, there are very specific nods to musical theater, especially certain shows. "The four grandparents of the show," McCarter quotes director Tommy Kail as saying, "are *Sweeney Todd, Jesus Christ Superstar, Evita,* and *Gypsy.*"

Kail explains, "*Gypsy* and *Sweeney* are the story of monsters…they're both about somebody who has already been judged by history, but the shows still creates mystery about why the monsters do what they do. *Evita* and *Jesus Christ Superstar* shows that music could lead the way" – they started as concept albums and were virtually sung through (*Hamilton: The Revolution*, 159).

Burr as narrator links with *Jesus Christ Superstar* and *Evita*, with the title character's nemesis as the narrator. These shows too emphasize that "who tells your story" is vital. Jesus and Judas have opposing political philosophies, as do Ché and Evita. The latter pair even keep running into each other. Mashing the pair together over and over intensifies the conflict and allows both sides of the philosophy a voice. As each criticizes the other's views, everyone's sainthood is shattered at least a bit. Finally, Burr, like Judas, can tell his side of the story but must take society's blame for his one defining murder.

In *Gypsy*, Rose and her two daughters, Baby June and Louise, are stuck in a sibling rivalry with the ultimate stage mom even as they seek clashing paths to fame. As Washington struggles to keep peace between Jefferson and Hamilton, among others, there are clear echoes. Far more, though, Hamilton is Rose, "Brash and politically insensitive, arrogant and brilliant, sometimes right but never in doubt" as he builds a great career then implodes it (Viertel 266). The first-act curtain leaves the characters flailing amid smashed dreams as they sing "Everything's Coming Up Roses." Likewise, "Yorktown" leaves the heroes of Hamilton winning the battle but floundering as King George warns them "What Comes Next" will be nearly impossible.

"Yorktown" is the "tent pole" as Viertel puts it, the song near the end of Act I that "keep[s] the roof from caving in on the audience," giving theatregoers a shot of energy so they'll stay attentive until intermission (142). The tent pole in Hamilton is "the entire American revolution." It's not a fun song per se, but "the kinetic excitement of watching a real showman figure out how to do a war in one extended number manages to thrill and reignite an audience that has already been sitting for a long time and processed a surprisingly large number of events" (Viertel 145).

Certainly *In the Heights* links with *Hamilton*. Lin-Manuel

Miranda did music and lyrics. Andy Blankenbuehler
choreographed it and Alex Lacamoire did the orchestrations.
Thomas Kail directed. It went from Off-Broadway to
Broadway and won several Tonys. Lin-Manuel Miranda and
Christopher Jackson starred. There are other connections:
Miranda originally gave himself the part of Usnavi, the
narrator, who begins by rapping exposition and introducing
the large ensemble in the opening number. In both of
Miranda's Broadway shows, there's a significant group of
multifaceted, fascinating characters – not just one or two.
Usnavi is young, scrappy, and ambitious like Hamilton or
Miranda himself. As he reveals early:

> my parents came with nothing
> They got a little more
> And sure, we're poor, but yo, at least we got the store
> And it's all about the legacy they left with me, it's destiny

Thus the play tackles the immigrant experience as well as the
all-important concept of legacy. Usnavi's conflict at the end
reflects Hamilton's at the beginning – leaving behind his
entire world to forge a new destiny elsewhere (ironically,
Usnavi considers leaving New York for the Caribbean). Both
must consider their definitions of success and both realize
near the end how lucky they've always been to be loved while
they were dreaming of far-off opportunities.

The play is set in Miranda's home neighborhood,
Washington Heights. As *Hamilton* does, it's a love letter to
New York. Both shows create parts for Latino and other
minority actors, welcoming the audience into modern
America and reproducing its sounds. Watching the audience,
Miranda noticed that every time hip-hop was used, everyone
sat up in their seats. "This mix of Latin music and hip-hop
was potent – there was something in that groove," he says
(Mead). Thus he carried the sound to his next show. Finally,
Miranda discovered to his delight that Eliza Hamilton
established the first school in Washington Heights. To him,
"it was a confirmation — I was supposed to do this"

(Browne). As he adds:

> And we had a line. And I put it in, where it was like "the first school" — and they went, in Washington Heights. I took the melody from my own shit in In the Heights, but it was just too on the nose. You just can't. Even though it's historically true, I can't actually say "in Washington Heights" at the end of my fucking show. But it was there to be mine. (Browne)

Les Mis was the first Broadway musical Miranda saw and an enormous influence (Miranda and McCarter, Hamilton: The Revolution 160). He notes, "I really got my Les Mis on in this score, like being really smart about where to reintroduce a theme. In terms of how it accesses your tear ducts, nothing does it better than that show" (Mead). The show is possibly the largest epic of musical theater, setting personal conflicts against a revolution, with many touching reprises. "The Story of Tonight" echoes "Drink with Me" as the men somberly plan a revolution, focusing on the core friendship (and drinking). There are more shared moments:

> He doesn't shy away from the blatant tear-jerking of Les Misérables magnitude in a couple of moments, such as the death scene of Hamilton's oldest son in 1801, shot in a duel defending his father from calumny, and wife Eliza's forgiveness of his philandering as they mourn their son together. (Solomon)

One clear homage in styles is the sympathetic villain. Like Javert and Jean Valjean in Les Mis, Burr and Hamilton are tied together as foils, so similar but for their opposing viewpoints. Both sets of characters meet early and grow old together, pursuing their rivalry against the backdrop of a greater war. Each has a gorgeous "I want" song establishing sympathy. In fact, Javert and Burr both have the same frustration – that they're following the rules of law and propriety but their rule-breaking nemesis is prospering, even though this isn't how the world should work. Each villain struggles because his life is so inextricably bound to the hero's.

There are subtler and quicker references as well – "The Room Where It Happens" echoes "Somewhere in a Tree," from Stephen Sondheim's *Pacific Overtures* score with a sinister jazz or blues feel. *The Pirates of Penzance* (Miranda's first high school production) shares multi-syllable rhymes and a trace of Gilbert and Sullivan's good natured humor – he calls them the "kings of light patter" (*Hamilton: The Revolution* 61).

George Washington (Christopher Jackson) borrows from *The Pirates of Penzance* when he calls himself the "model of a modern major general"; Hamilton invokes *The Last Five Years* when he pays off his blackmailer, telling him, "Nobody needs to know." Burr gets in two references in a single rhyme as he urges his rebel colleagues to stay calm: "The situation is fraught" (*A Funny Thing Happened on the Way to the Forum*). "You've got to be carefully taught" (*South Pacific*'s liberal outcry against racism). Quoting *1776*, Hamilton cries, "Sit down, John!" (adding an obscene epithet) as he drops his infamous screed pamphlet against John Adams onto the floor. (Solomon)

Miranda calls "The Schuyler Sisters" "our 'One Short Day in the Emerald City'" number and "a love letter to New York" (*Hamilton: The Revolution* 44). Since Burr and Hamilton go from frenemies to friends to political enemies, there's a lot of the witches' story from *Wicked* here, even as both musicals deconstruct good guys, bad guys, and the choice of narrator. The witches end acknowledging what each has taught the other – this happens through the course of the second act for Burr and Hamilton as each tries the other's strategy of waiting or seizing the day to succeed politically.

Finally, Miranda harks back to the golden-age musical and its perky optimism, seen in the sisters' "Look around look around at how/Lucky we are to be alive right now." The shows might have dark moments but ended happily with a celebration and triumph. "Hamilton recalls the spirit of shows staged before edginess and angst were brought into the genre by the likes of Stephen Sondheim or Kander and Ebb—back, that is, to the day when, like American politics,

Broadway musicals also followed a commandment to be optimistic and uplifting" (Solomon). Back in the fifties, sugary musicals and their songs blossomed.

> When rock rumbled onto the scene, a great disruption took place; the art of crafting a song in which lyrics and music blended seamlessly, and were married in service of character and story, was suddenly irrelevant, or relevant only to those who had grown up with the form. In rock, as in much opera, music almost always predominates. Lyrics often become a scattered, sometimes nonsensical shout from the soul – or the loins. (Isherwood)

At the time, *Hair* became the only truly successful musical to incorporate rock music. As Miranda exclaims, "It's so crazy that *Hair* came out in the fucking Sixties, and still, anytime there's a rock musical, it's like [stuffy voice], "Does rock belong on Broadway?" (Binelli). Other shows like the bitter, world-weary *A Chorus Line* succeeded, as did John Kander and Fred Ebb's cynical *Chicago*.

"Breglio dates the beginning of this "uneasy alliance" between commercial and non-commercial theatre to *A Chorus Line*, which had its initial run at the nonprofit Public Theater and transferred to Broadway in 1975, where it became a phenomenal success, generating millions of dollars" (Mandell). *Hamilton*, of course, got its start at the same place. The cast even held a celebration for the fortieth anniversary of *A Chorus Line* there and sang "What I Did For Love," then invited up the original cast. The owner of the Public Theater described how *A Chorus Line* focused on the backgrounds of the contributors rather than the star, and compared it to *Hamilton*, a story with the same message, "told by the people who actually make up this country" ("Hamilton - A Chorus Line Celebration").

> And then, suddenly, the British (and French) were coming – this time to the rescue. The pop operas of Andrew Lloyd Webber (*Cats* and *The Phantom of the Opera*) and Claude-

Michel Schönberg and Alain Boublil (*Les Misérables* and
Miss Saigon) dominated the scene during the 1980s, the
lone force, it sometimes seemed, countering the decadence
into which the Broadway musical had slipped, like a
washed-up diva listening endlessly to her old recordings.
(Isherwood)

The 2000s offered some more original stories with edgy
Spring Awakening and the breakout hit *Wicked* and Miranda's
Tony Award-winning *In the Heights*, with the rapping that set
the stage (as it were) for *Hamilton*. In much more recent days,
musicals have been flooding the big and small screens, from
big budget movies of many of the latter shows to *High School
Musical* and the TV series *Glee*. These "made musical theater
'hip' again for those who had outgrown the Disney movie
years" (Isherwood). Thus the world, and especially the young
audience, were primed for a new, groundbreaking twist on
the tradition.

Miranda reveals that he keeps tinkering, hoping for
something truly spectacular. "Because those are the shows we
love. We love *Fiddler*. We love *West Side Story*. I want to be in
that club. I want to be in the club that writes the musical that
every high school does. We're this close" (MagGregor).
Indeed, many critics are already anticipating all the teens who
will perform *Hamilton* as a classic for their era, a musical
written with tons of minority parts that's edgy but also makes
history fun.

On Broadway, there's the Hamilton Effect – people,
having enjoyed the one musical, buy tickets to more or get
subscriptions. This is especially apparent among young
people in their twenties and thirties. Of course, a similar surge
has occurred many times with breakout smashes like *The Book
of Mormon* or *Wicked* or *The Lion King*. *Billboard* called the
Hamilton album the Best Rap Album of the Year in 2015,
suggesting it could mainstream Broadway – returning to the
days when songs from musicals appeared on the radio as
popular music.

Rap/Hip-hop

"The hip-hop narrative is writing your way out of your circumstances" Miranda explains ("Hamilton: A Founding Father"). It often communicates a personal belief system and a contextualized view of the world as it really is. It challenges and demands change. Always on the attack, it calls things the way they are. Thus it's a wonderful reimagining of the history. "It wants to talk about life in America as it really is lived on the margins of society and chronicle the struggle to move toward the center of power" (Viertel 266).

> Lyrics allude to rap stars and their songs—there are verbal hat tips to Mobb Deep, the Fugees, Grandmaster Flash, Brand Nubian, and especially the Notorious BIG (whose "Ten Crack Commandments" is remade into "Duel Commandments," which dynamically explains the protocol for affairs of honor). (Solomon)

The opening number has the call-and-response of "What's your name?" – a mode familiar from hits from everyone from Snoop Dogg to DMX to Rihanna and Drake. Meanwhile, the rising harmonies as the chorus sings "New York" are reminiscent of Jay Z and Alicia Keys' "Empire State of Mind" (Wickman).

Hercules Mulligan, John Laurens, and the Marquis de Lafayette introduce themselves by crying, "What time is it? Showtime!" the way the Litefeet dancers enter the New York subway. Mulligan's "Brrrap, brrrap," is common in rap, imitating machine gun fire. Thus he gets a blatantly contemporary moment.

> "When you're developing your voice as a rapper, you figure out your cadence – your swag – and that's how you write," Bay Area rapper Daveed Diggs [Lafayette/Jefferson] says. "Lin managed to figure that out for all of these different characters – everyone has their own swag, and it feels germane to them. And that's really impressive. Hercules Mulligan raps exactly like a dude named Hercules Mulligan!" (Binelli)

VALERIE ESTELLE FRANKEL

"I'm John Laurens in the place to be" is "a love letter to
old school hip-hop" and a staple of rap (*Hamilton: The
Revolution* 25). "My Shot" "carries the DNA of 'Shook
Ones'" (*Hamilton: The Revolution* 95). "I'm only 19, but my
mind is older" is a Mobb Deep line. In the line there's also a
Mobb Deep shrill tone hip-hop fans recognize. Hamilton
spells out his name proudly, adding the cadence of Notorious
B.I.G. in "Going Back to Cali." A Tupac reference appears
with "I gotta holler just to be heard." Big Pun likes a string of
rhymes and Miranda uses those too with lines like "between
all the bleedin' 'n fightin'/I've been readin' 'n writin'."

"Right Hand Man" has the ensemble calling "What" "in
what sounds like a very precise imitation of one of DMX's
signature ad libs in songs like "Party Up in Here" (Wickman).
The repeating "Boom goes the cannon" is from Busta
Rhymes' part in "Scenario."

Miranda calls Burr's "Excuse me, miss, I know it's not
funny/But your perfume smells like your daddy's got money"
in "The Schuyler Sisters" "our little Jay Z/Pharrel homage"
(*Hamilton: The Revolution* 44).

The section of "Right Hand Man" in which George
Washington is courting Hamilton to come work by his side
reminded me of "Coming of Age," from Jay Z's debut
album, "Reasonable Doubt." It's a back-and-forth between
him and a hungry protégé, Memphis Bleek. Jay is looking
for an eager student, and I can imagine Bleek coming back
at him with Hamilton's refrain: "I am not throwing away my
shot." (Tommasini and Caramanica)

The ball where Hamilton meets Eliza has some of the
men calling out for the "laaaadies" in an echo of the Beastie
Boys' "Hey Ladies." Hamilton's own growl in "Helpless" is
an homage to JaRule and his duets, included because it makes
his costar laugh. "Meet Me Inside" repeats the title phrase,
apparently inverting a repeated "meet me outside" (with the
same rhythm) in DMX's "Party Up in Here." Busta Rhymes
goes from soft to suddenly loud, and "Yorktown" imitates

144

this.

> "Guns and Ships" sounds like a nod to a classic Eminem
> song as Hamilton, Lafayette, Burr and Washington discuss
> the war and the effort that goes into fighting one. It's also
> the speediest record on Broadway with 19 words per
> second. ("Going H.A.M.")

"There's a bit of the hip-hop classic 'The Message' in
'What'd I Miss'" (Tommasini and Caramanica). Likewise, the
cheating song "Say No to This," starts with a quote from LL
Cool J's "I Need Love."

Of course, the rap battles, with speedy, free-flowing
insults, certainly spice up the political debate:

> A confrontational cadence is the warp and woof of rap.
> Even the most "conscious," constructive, or even puckish
> rappers retain a chip-on-the-shoulder tone in their delivery
> (not accidentally termed "spitting" among fans). Each rhyme
> at the end of a line implies a "So, there!" Rapping is, to an
> extent, sport. This works so well in Hamilton because most
> of the characters are men in competition. It isn't an accident
> that two debates between Hamilton and Jefferson,
> amenable to recasting as rap battles, are among the high
> points of the show. But argument, topping, and display are
> only one part of being human—or of being a character in a
> musical. (McWhorter 51)

The rap battle opens with its moderator, George
Washington, introducing the event: "Ladies and gentlemen,
you could've been anywhere in the world tonight, but you're
here with us in New York City!" This echoes Jay Z's "Izzo
(H.O.V.A.)." Also, Thomas Jefferson begins his second verse
with an homage to Grandmaster Flash's landmark single
"The Message." He tells Hamilton he doesn't have the votes,
he adds a little "ah ha ha ha," and then smirks, "Such a
blunder/Sometimes it makes me wonder/why I even bring
the thunder." In "The Message," the refrain is "It's like a
jungle/Sometimes it makes me wonder/How I keep from
going under/Ah ha ha ha." Musical director Alex Lacamoire

explained

> That first rap battle, it's more old-school. He even does that Grandmaster Flash reference: "a-ha-ha-ha-ha." Whereas the second one just has the cool Neptunes, Pharrell vibe to it. The bass is very round, it doesn't have a lot of bite to it, and the drums are super Neptunes-y, like, *boom-kat, boom-ta-tic-cacko!* (Jones)

In the second cabinet battle, there's Biggie reference from "Juicy," with Jefferson's "And if you don't know, now you know, Mr. President." The original line has something much racier for the address. "Set to a Harlem Shake-ready beat, the disagreement finds George Washington trying to moderate and diffuse tensions between the two" ("Going H.A.M."). Meanwhile, Hamilton grins triumphantly as he dances about, taking a fundamental joy in the competition – another hallmark of rap battles.

"It's Quiet Uptown" is reminiscent of "Biggie's 'Suicidal Thoughts,' still one of the most chilling hip-hop songs of all time," as the hero and heroine "confront [their] own mortality... [and] end up exhausted, frayed, desperate" (Tommasini and Caramanica).

All these musical shout-outs emphasize that American history can be reimagined and reclaimed.

> Might *Hamilton* augur something more? For 125 years, American musical theatre language has been driven by serial infusions of black pop energy, creating the sound of Broadway so familiar today, including manifestations now processed as thoroughly "white." Given that hip-hop has been the mainstream for young Americans of all colors for at least 20 years, isn't this when we would expect Broadway music to come in for its next injection of, as it were, "flava" and evolve into a whole new direction? Actually, not. The pitfalls of presentism acknowledged, it is worth venturing that rap is crucially different from the musical genres that transformed show music in the past. Rap is likely to take its place in Broadway music but not transform it, because for all of its glories, rap offers more

limited dramatic possibilities than ragtime, jazz, or even rock. (McWhorter 48)

Miranda has been part of the comedy/improv rap troupe Freestyle Love Supreme for years, along with George Washington, Christopher Jackson. Thus his association with the style goes far back and he was determined to get it right. At the client meeting for *Hamilton*, Miranda writes, he told the SpotCo designers he didn't want any artwork featuring the founding fathers in gold chains "or any other hackneyed hip-hop trope that people who have no idea about hip-hop think hiphop is" (Mandell). He explains of the show:

I built this score by dream casting my favorite artists. I always imagined George Washington as a mix between Common and John Legend (a pretty good description of Christopher Jackson, actually, who plays our first president); Hercules Mulligan was Busta Rhymes; and Hamilton was modeled after my favorite polysyllabic rhyming heroes, Rakim, Big Pun and Eminem. In *Hamilton*, we're telling the stories of old, dead white men but we're using actors of color, and that makes the story more immediate and more accessible to a contemporary audience. You don't distance the audience by putting an actor of color in a role that you would think of as default Caucasian. No, you excite people and you draw them in. (DiGiacomo)

On first reading the biography, Hamilton actually reminded Miranda of Tupac Shakur, the West Coast rapper who was shot to death in 1996. "Shakur was also extremely undiplomatic, publicly calling out rappers he hated. Miranda recognized a similar rhetorical talent in Hamilton, and a similar, fatal failure to know when enough was enough" (Mead).

Finally, Miranda discusses meeting some of these great rappers:

Busta was the first and the greatest, because he sat in the front row. That was about as nervous as I've been. For me,

it's been exciting to meet a lot of lyrical giants. Andre 3000, when he came, I was very conscious of him. Eminem was another one of those. I was sick when Jay Z and Beyoncé came, so I missed that particular pleasure of performing for them. When Nas came, I was a wreck. I actually gave him my copy of the Chernow book that I took on vacation! It was very impulsive. It's always interesting when your heroes react in a way that's in keeping with what you think of them. Nas' reaction to the show was "I want to read more about this era," because Nas is our hip-hop scholar and intellectual. So I just gave him the book! [Laughs]
...
Eminem was really cool. He asked, "What happens if you mess up?" [Laughs] And I said, "I messed up three times because I knew you were here!" Will Smith was a big one. LL Cool J was a real interesting one. I'd met LL before he came, because I had a friend who was on that NCIS show. I remember asking him at the time, "Are you going to make any new music?" And he said to me – this is a great quote and it's always sort of stayed with me – "I don't want to make something that isn't a classic." But the way he said it was, "I want to work in marble." That really stuck with me. So when he came to the show, I said, "I tried to work in marble, sir." (Binelli)

The Apocrypha
What's been interesting is that *Hamilton* has proliferated in the age of social media. I believe the magic of theater is that we are all in the same room having the same experience. I think people really crave that communal experience. But I also saw what happened when the cast album came out. It was first streamed for free on NPR, and people started freaking out when they heard it then, and then it was on sale later that week. And streaming it for free didn't hurt the sales at all—it whetted people's appetite. So that was fascinating. (Kokalitcheva)

As Miranda thus considers how *Twitter* and radio have aided spreading the word, he takes his show into a new century. Since his White House rap first spread the word of his show when it reached *YouTube*, it's not surprising he claims social media for his show and finds ways to use it to connect with fans. His second White House performance is also on *YouTube*, as are a few solo scenes from the show.

Another beloved add-on is the #Ham4Ham experience.
Miranda explains:

> Our plan was always to have a lottery outside the theater for the front row, sell the front row seats for $10. Ham for Ham: You pay a Hamilton to see Hamilton. And 700 people showed up to our first lottery drawing—that is an insane amount of people. I was there watching this crowd grow. I got a megaphone and said, "Thank you so much for coming, I love you very much, goodbye." And my collaborator Tommy Kail said, "There's 20 people who got the tickets and 680 people who are just going to be sent disappointed into the streets of New York. You should grab the megaphone before every lottery drawing." That became the #Ham4Ham show and this de facto talent show. I brought in actors from other theaters and some of my musical theater heroes. It could be anything from Jonathan Groff and I singing songs we sang in middle school to dancers from the New York City Ballet doing a solo in the streets of New York. And then as people filmed that, and that went online, that became this extra experience for fans.
>
> What we created almost by accident is this community of people who are very invested in the show and invested in the people who work on the show, and also the sort of "only in New York" moments that we create outside the box office. (Kokalitcheva)

In fact, hundreds of fans crowd *Hamilton*'s live "Ham4Ham" lottery each Wednesday, hoping to win one of 21 last-minute $10 tickets to see that day's show, and tens of thousands per day try their luck at the online lotto. Some of these shows are on *YouTube* as well.

However, many aren't lucky enough to live in New York or even the other cities where the show is touring. For these fans, there are a few other options. In October 2015, the Original Broadway Cast Recording debuted at No. 12 on the Billboard charts—the highest starting position for a Broadway show in 50 years—and in November it became the first to top the rap charts.

October 17, 2016, PBS' *Great Performances* aired a 90-minute documentary produced by Miranda, titled *Hamilton's*

America. It features many film clips of the musical along with cast interviews, history, and backstory. Miranda also tours many of the historical sites connected with the story.

Fans supplement the music with Miranda's *Hamilton: The Revolution*, a hardcover book that includes the annotated libretto, behind-the-scenes photos and the musical's origin story. Many of Miranda's thoughts and comments offer background not available to theatergoers. It's been on the New York Times hardcover nonfiction best-seller list since its April release, alongside its paperback cousin *Alexander Hamilton,* the decade-old, 800-page Ron Chernow biography that inspired the show (Berman).

Another offering is *The Hamilton Mixtape:*

> Now that he's brought hip-hop to Broadway, Miranda can't help dreaming of bringing Broadway back to the radio. "You used to hear a Cole Porter song on the radio," he says, "and then you'd go pay for a ticket to a Broadway show to hear that song in a show." He's enlisted the Roots' Questlove to try to make a cast album that sounds more like Hot 97 than the ultraclean, vocals-über alles sound of other Broadway LPs. "If any cast album could afford to push the limit of that," says Miranda, "it's this one." (Hiatt)

Kelly Clarkson, Usher, Alicia Keys, Queen Latifa, Chance the Rapper, The Roots, John Legend, Nas, Sia, Jill Scott, Ashanti, and Wiz Khalifa were among its stars. Miranda joins in on the rap "Wrote My Way Out." As Miranda adds of his new pet project:

> It's about turning to those rap gods and heroes and saying, "What in the show inspires you? Go make something." And we're not being very doctrinaire about it. Right now, and this could change because we're still making tracks, but it's about a 50-50 mix of covers and inspired-bys. So for every song where it's an artist covering the song verbatim, as it appears in the show, there's a song where you take the hook of "Right Hand Man," but it's two rappers invoking the theme of "Right Hand Man" and doing what they want with it. There's a version of "Who Lives, Who Dies, Who Tells

Your Story" that's not about Eliza, it's about who lives, who
dies and who tells your story. (Binelli)

Jill Scott sings "Say Yes to This," flipping Miranda's concept,
while Wiz Khalifa adapts one to "Washingtons on Your
Side." K'naan, Snow Tha Product, Riz MC, and Residente riff
on Miranda's beloved line with "Immigrants (We Get the Job
Done)." A few cut numbers make it in as well.

At the Richard Rodgers Theater, a day before the release
of the album, musicians including Black Thought, Regina
Spektor, Ashanti and Ja Rule performed songs from the
mixtape, a show available on *YouTube* (#Ham4Ham 12/1).
The Hamilton Mixtape entered the Billboard 200 at No. 1.

The Future

A second production will open on Oct. 19 in Chicago, its
first six months of shows selling faster than you can say
"Federalist papers." A touring production plans to launch in
March in San Francisco before hitting nearly 20 other U.S.
cities, and the show will go global next fall when another
offshoot is set to open on London's West End. "I've been
doing this job for over 20 years, and there's never been
another show remotely comparable in terms of advance
excitement, demand, tickets, general enthusiasm," says
Chicago Tribune chief theater critic Chris Jones. "When
tickets went on sale here, it was front page of our paper.
Frankly, it's just nuts—unfathomable almost."
(Berman)

Miranda leaves the titular role to Javier Munoz, his
understudy since *In the Heights*. Munoz has played the lead
character once a week since the show's 2015 launch and in
front of some notable attendees, among them President
Barack Obama, Beyoncé and Jay Z.

Miranda isn't sure exactly what his next step will be.
There are some stand-alone album projects he'd like to do,
and there's always the temptation of Hollywood.

"It's tricky for me," he says. "I have a couple of ideas for
films. But, you know, Quentin Tarantino acted in a play, and
I'm very happy that he got that opportunity, but I also want

him to keep making movies because he's one of the best people in the world at making movies! I have these other interests, but I've worked really hard to get good at writing shows, so it's not a matter of stopping that to do other things. It's a matter of how much else can I fit in my life." (Hiatt)

As for *Hamilton*'s other departing stars, Leslie Odom Jr. (Burr) released a self-titled jazz album on S-Curve Records/BMG. Phillipa Soo (Eliza) will star in Broadway's *Amelie* musical. Tony winners Renée Elise Goldsberry and Daveed Diggs, as well as Christopher Jackson, Okieriete Onaodowan, Anthony Ramos and Jasmine Cephas Jones, are likely renewing their contracts while juggling other projects (Lee).

As Miranda reveals, the true power of the show is its ability to educate about a modern America of equality. He explains:

> What I can tell you is that works of art are the only silver bullet we have against racism and sexism and hatred. Joe Biden happened to see *Hamilton* on the same day James Burrows was here. James Burrows directed every episode of *Will & Grace*, and remember when Biden went on *Meet the Press* and essentially said, "Yeah, gay people should get married"? He very openly credited *Will & Grace* with changing the temperature on how we discuss gays and lesbians in this country. It was great to see Jim Burrows and Joe Biden talk about that, and Jim thanked Biden and Biden thanked Jim because that was a piece of art changing the temperature of how we talked about a divisive issue. It sounds silly. It's a sitcom, but that doesn't make it not true. Art engenders empathy in a way that politics doesn't, and in a way that nothing else really does. Art creates change in people's hearts. But it happens slowly. (DiGiacomo)

With *Hamilton* around, it may happen a little faster.

APPENDIX

VALERIE ESTELLE FRANKEL

SONGS

Hamilton Album: Act 1
Alexander Hamilton
Aaron Burr, Sir
My Shot
Story Of Tonight
Schuyler Sisters
Farmer Refuted
You'll Be Back
Right Hand Man
A Winter's Ball
Helpless
Satisfied
The Story of Tonight (Reprise)
Wait For It
Stay Alive
Ten Duel Commandments
Meet Me Inside
That Would Be Enough
Guns and Ships
History Has Its Eyes On You
Yorktown (The World Turned Upside Down)
What Comes Next
Dear Theodosia
Non-Stop

Hamilton Album: Act 2
What'd I Miss
Cabinet Battle #1
Take A Break
Say No To This
Room Where It Happens
Schuyler Defeated
Cabinet Battle #2

Washington On Your Side
One Last Time
I Know Him
The Adams Administration
We Know
Hurricane
The Reynolds Pamphlet
Burn
Blow Us All Away
Stay Alive (Reprise)
It's Quiet Uptown
Election of 1800
Your Obedient Servant
Best of Wives and Best of Women
The World Was Wide Enough
Who Lives, Who Dies, Who Tells Your Story

ORIGINAL CAST AND CREATORS 2015-2016

The world premiere of "Hamilton" was presented in New York in February 2015 by The Public Theater (Off-Broadway). It moved to the Richard Rodgers Theatre on Broadway August 6, 2015.

Book by Lin-Manuel Miranda; Music by Lin-Manuel Miranda; Lyrics by Lin-Manuel Miranda
Inspired by the book *Alexander Hamilton* by Ron Chernow
Music Direction and Orchestrations by Alex Lacamoire; Arrangements by Alex Lacamoire and Lin-Manuel Miranda
Directed by Thomas Kail
Choreography by Andy Blankenbuehler
Scenic Design by David Korins
Costume Design by Paul Tazewell
Lighting Design by Howell Binkley
Sound Design by Nevin Steinberg
Hair and Wig Design by Charles G. LaPointe

Cast
Alexander Hamilton...Lin-Manuel Miranda
Aaron Burr...Leslie Odom, Jr.
Eliza Schuyler Hamilton...Phillipa Soo
Angelica Schuyler...Renée Elise Goldsberry
Marquis de Lafayette/Thomas Jefferson... Daveed Diggs
George Washington...Christopher Jackson
King George III...Brian d'Arcy James (Off-Broadway)
King George III...Jonathan Groff (Broadway)
John Laurens / Philip Hamilton...Anthony Ramos
Peggy Schuyler / Maria Reynolds...Jasmine Cephas Jones
Hercules Mulligan / James Madison...Okieriete Onaodowan

VALERIE ESTELLE FRANKEL

WORKS CITED

Alexander Hamilton: American Experience, written by Ronald Blumer, produced and directed by Muffie Meyer, PBS, 2007. http://www.pbs.org/wgbh/amex/hamilton/filmmore/pt.html.

Berman, Eliza. "Hamilton Nation." *Time,* vol. 188, no. 14, 2016, pp. 50. *MasterFILE Premier.*

Binelli, Mark. "Hamilton Mania." *Rolling Stone,* vol. 1263, 2016, pp. 36. MasterFILE Premier.

Bradner, Eric. "Pence: 'I wasn't offended' by Message of *Hamilton* Cast." *CNN Politics,* 20 Nov. 2016. http://www.cnn.com/2016/11/20/politics/mike-pence-hamilton-message-trump.

Browne, Rembert. "Genius: A Conversation With 'Hamilton' Maestro Lin-Manuel Miranda." *Grantland.* http://grantland.com/hollywood-prospectus/genius-a-conversation-with-hamilton-maestro-lin-manuel-miranda.

Chernow, Ron. *Alexander Hamilton.* Penguin Books, 2005.

Corde, Phoebe. "The Piece of Foreshadowing in *Hamilton* That Everyone Misses." *Odyssey,* 19 Sept 2016. https://www.theodysseyonline.com/piece-foreshadowing-hamilton-misses.

DiGiacomo, Frank. "*Hamilton's* Lin-Manuel Miranda on Finding Originality, Racial Politics (and Why Trump Should See His Show)" Hollywood Reporter, 12 Aug. 2015. http://www.hollywoodreporter.com/features/hamiltons-lin-manuel-miranda-finding-814657.

Dreamcatcher. "All Deleted Songs from *Hamilton*." 6 Dec. 2016. https://www.youtube.com/watch?v=EZkANYGycNU.

"The Duel," *The American Experience, PBS.org,* 2000. http://www.pbs.org/wgbh/amex/duel/filmmore/refere nce/interview/freeman08.html

Eddy, Michael S. "A Scaffold to Build a Nation On." *Stage Directions,* vol. 28, no.10, 2015, pp. 10. *MasterFILE Premier.*

Eggert, Jessica. "'Satisfied' Lyrics: Reviews and Meaning Behind *Hamilton* Musical Song." *Mic.com,* 22 Oct. 2015. https://mic.com/articles/127218/satisfied-lyrics-reviews- and-meaning-behind-hamilton-musical-song.

Evans, Suzy. "The Room Where It Happens." *American Theatre,* vol. 32, no. 7, 2015, pp. 26. *MasterFILE Premier.*

Feller, Alison. "Hamilton Makes History." *Dance Spirit,* vol. 20, no. 6, 2016, pp. 46. *MasterFILE Premier.*

"Going H.A.M.: A Track-By-Track Review of the *Hamilton* Soundtrack." *Vibe,* Oct. 2015. http://www.vibe.com/2015/10/hamilton-soundtrack- review.

Fleming, Thomas. *Duel: Alexander Hamilton, Aaron Burr, and the Future of America.* New York: Basic Books, 1999.

#Ham4Ham 12/1 – The Hamilton Mixtape Performance." *YouTube,* uploaded by *Hamilton: An American Musical,* 1 Dec. 2016. https://www.youtube.com/watch?v=GdAjETiwtSk

"Hamilton - A Chorus Line Celebration." *YouTube,* uploaded by Playbill Video, 14 Aug 2015.

"Hamilton." *Drunk History.* Comedy Central, 29 Nov. 2016. https://www.youtube.com/watch?v=86mukiciQ6E.

"Hamilton: A Founding Father Takes to the Stage." *YouTube,* uploaded by *CBS Sunday Morning,* 8 Mar. 2015. https://www.youtube.com/watch?v=0wboCdgzLHg.

Hamilton, Alexander. "Letter to Edward Carrington." *TeachingAmericanHistory.org,* May 26, 1792. http://teachingamericanhistory.org/library/document/le tter-to-edward-carrington/

–. *The Papers of Alexander Hamilton,* edited by Harold C. Syrett. Columbia University, 1961.

"Hamilton Parody - Hillary Rodham Clinton!" The Key of

Awesome #114. *YouTube*, uploaded by The Key of Awesome, 27 Oct. 2016 https://www.youtube.com/watch?v=EWtIGEZevDw

Hamilton's America. PBS, 21 Oct. 2016.

Hiatt, Brian. "Broadway's Hip-Hop Masterpiece." *Rolling Stone*, vol. 1245, 2015, pp. 46. *MasterFILE Premier*.

"Hip-hop and History Blend for Broadway hit *Hamilton*." *YouTube*, uploaded by *PBS NewsHour*, 20 Nov. 2015. https://www.youtube.com/watch?v=HAiEVjW-GNA

Isenberg, Nancy. *Fallen Founder: The Life of Aaron Burr*. Viking, 2007.

Isherwood, Charles. "Printing Money." *Opera News*, vol. 81, no. 4, 2016, pp. 34. *MasterFILE Premier*.

James, Kendra. "Race, Immigration, and Hamilton: The Relevance of Lin-Manuel Miranda's New Musical." *The Toast*, 1 Oct., 2015. http://the-toast.net/2015/10/01/race-immigration-and-hamilton.

John Adams. Directed by Tom Hooper. HBO, 2008.

Johnson, Paul. *History of the American People*. Harper Perennial, 1999.

Jones, Nate. "Nerding Out With Hamilton Musical Director, Alex Lacamoire," *Vulture*, 13 Jan 2016. http://www.vulture.com/2016/01/hamilton-alex-lacamoire-interview.html.

Jung, Carl. "The Archetypes and the Collective Unconscious." *Collected Works*, translated by R.F.C. Hull, Bollingen Series XX, Princeton University Press, 1969.

–. "Civilization in Transition." *Collected Works*, translated by R.F.C. Hull, Bollingen Series XX, Princeton University Press, 1969.

–. "Concerning the Archetypes, with Special Reference to the Anima Concept," *Collected Works*, translated by R.F.C. Hull, Bollingen Series XX, Princeton University Press, 1969.

Kokalitcheva, Kia. "Hamilton, Nonstop." *Fortune*, vol. 174 no. 5, 2016, pp. 74-75. *Business Source Elite*.

Kowalski, Kathiann M. "Hamilton On Stage!" *Cobblestone*, vol.

37 no. 8, 2016, pp. 34. *MasterFILE Premier.*

Lee, Ashley. "What's Next For Hamilton?" *Billboard,* vol. 128, no. 17, 2016, pp. 16. *Business Source Elite.*

"Lin-Manuel Miranda Monologue – SNL." *YouTube,* uploaded by *Saturday Night Live,* 8 Oct 2016. https://www.youtube.com/watch?v=AsupmN90wBk.

"Lin-Manuel Miranda Performing the John Adams Rap that was Cut from the Musical Hamilton. Amazing." *YouTube,* uploaded by sticars's channel, 14 Mar. 2015. https://www.youtube.com/watch?v=oUI8b17YGx8.

Lomask, Milton. *Aaron Burr: The Years from Princeton to Vice President, 1756–1805.* Farrar, Straus and Giroux, 1979.

Maggregor, Jeff. "The Maestro." *Smithsonian,* vol. 46, no. 8, 2015, pp. 52. *MasterFILE Premier.*

Mandell, Jonathan. "The Very Model of a Modern Major Musical." *American Theatre,* vol. 33, no. 7, 2016, pp. 46. *MasterFILE Premier.*

"Matthew Broderick Joins Conan's *Hamilton* Parody, *Camelton* - CONAN on TBS Team." *YouTube,* uploaded by Coco, 4 Nov 2016. https://www.youtube.com/watch?v=VEqVlb0O8U4

Matteson, Addie. "Teaching With Hamilton." *School Library Journal,* vol. 62, no. 5, 2016, pp. 44. *MasterFILE Premier.*

McWhorter, John. "Will *Hamilton* Save The Musical? Don't Wait For It." *American Theatre,* vol. 33, no. 3, 2016, pp. 48. *MasterFILE Premier.*

Mead, Rebecca. "All About the Hamiltons." *The New Yorker,* 9 Feb. 2015. http://www.newyorker.com/magazine/2015/02/09/hamiltons

Miranda, Lin-Manuel. "Your Stories Are Essential." *Vital Speeches of the Day,* vol. 82, no. 8, 2016, pp. 245-247. *Academic Search Premier.*

Miranda, Lin-Manuel and Jeremy McCarter. *Hamilton: The Revolution.* Hachette Book Group, 2016.

Obama, Barak. "Remarks Prior to a Musical Performance by Members of the Cast of "Hamilton." *Daily Compilation of*

Presidential Documents, 2016, pp. 1. MasterFILE Premier.

Smith, Kyle. "Dueling Misfits." *New Criterion* vol. 34, no. 2, 2015, pp. 39. *MasterFILE Premier*.

Solomon, Alisa. "A Modern Major Musical." *Nation*, vol. 301, no. 11/12, 2015, pp. 27. *MasterFILE Premier*.

Stasio, Marilyn. "*Hamilton* Review: Lin-Manuel Miranda's Musical at the Public Theater – Variety." *Variety*, 2015. http://variety.com/2015/legit/reviews/review-hamilton-public-theater-lin-manuel-miranda-1201435257.

Tommasini, Anthony and Jon Caramanica "Exploring 'Hamilton' and Hip-Hop Steeped in Heritage." *The New York Times*, 30 Aug. 2015. http://www.nytimes.com/2015/08/30/theater/explorin g-hamilton-and-hip-hop-steeped-in-heritage.html.

"Trump vs. *Hamilton* Inspires a Hip Hop Musical Spin-Off" *YouTube*, uploaded *by The Late Show with Stephen Colbert*, 22 Nov. 2016. https://www.youtube.com/watch?v=T2p20sSiJcs

Viertel, Jack. *The Secret Life of the American Musical*. Sarah Crichton Books, 2016.

Wallace, David Duncan. *The Life of Henry Laurens*. G.P. Putnam's Sons, 1915. Archive.org. https://archive.org/details/lifeofhenrylaure00walluoft.

Wickman, Forrest. "All the Hip-Hop References in Hamilton: A Track-by-Track Guide." *Slate*, 24 Sept. 2015. http://www.slate.com/blogs/browbeat/2015/09/24/ha milton_s_hip_hop_references_all_the_rap_and_r_b_allus ions_in_lin_manuel.html.

VALERIE ESTELLE FRANKEL

ABOUT THE AUTHOR

Valerie Estelle Frankel is the author of many books on pop culture, including *Doctor Who – The What, Where, and How, Sherlock: Every Canon Reference You May Have Missed in BBC's Series 1-3,* and *How Game of Thrones Will End.* Many of her books focus on women's roles in fiction, from her heroine's journey guides *From Girl to Goddess* and *Buffy and the Heroine's Journey* to books like *Women in Game of Thrones* and *The Many Faces of Katniss Everdeen.* Once a lecturer at San Jose State University, she now teaches at Mission College. Come explore her research at www.vefrankel.com.

Made in the USA
Coppell, TX
17 September 2020